On the Road Again

Photo Essays on Famous Literary Sites in Japan

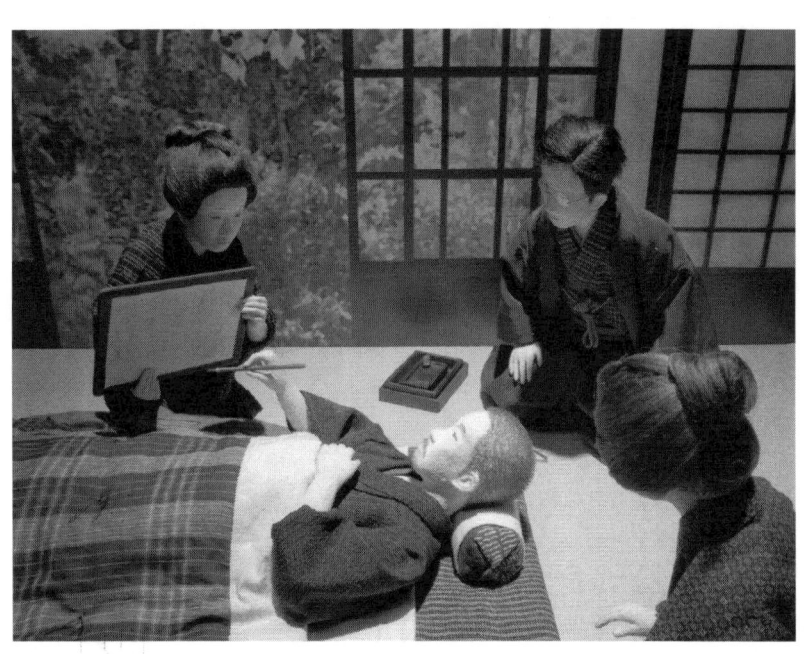

John J. Han

Copyright© John J. Han

ISBN: 978-93-89690-69-9

First Edition: 2020

Rs. 200/-

Cyberwit.net
HIG 45 Kaushambi Kunj, Kalindipuram
Allahabad - 211011 (U.P.) India
http://www.cyberwit.net
Tel: +(91) 9415091004 +(91) (532) 2552257
E-mail: info@cyberwit.net

No part of this book may be reproduced or transmitted in any form or by any means, electronic, mechanical, photocopying, or otherwise, without the express written consent of John J. Han.

Printed at Thomson Press (India) Ltd.

Table of Contents

Acknowledgments   4

Foreword
   By C. Clark Triplett, Ph.D.   6

Introductory Notes   10
   Note on the Front Cover Photo   16
   Note on the Back Cover Photo   17

Photo Essays
Haiku Pilgrimage to Tokyo   19
A Short Life, a Big Presence: Ichiyo Higuchi Sites in Tokyo   33
Natsume Soseki Sites at or near the University of Tokyo   43
Peace and Tranquility: Literary Treasures in Kyoto   53
Kamakura Museum of Literature   81
Yamanakako Forest Park of Literature   91
Shiki and Soseki Sites in Matsuyama, the "Haiku Capital"   101
Onomichi, Fumiko Hayashi's Home during Her Teenage
   Years   113
Gem of Japanese Literature: The Path of Literature in
   Onomichi   121
In Search of Kawabata's Dancer: The Izu Peninsula   131

Reader Response Essays
The Threads of Life
   By Mason Arledge   144
Mountains and Fireflies
   By Clayton Varley   149
Keeping Readers Interested
   By Grace Hahn   153

About the Author   156

Acknowledgments

It was a pleasure to share the chapters in progress with my fellow members of On the Edge (Jefferson County Library—Windsor Branch) and Write along Workshop (St. Louis County Library—Indian Trails). Special thanks go to Clark Triplett for his foreword and to Mason Arledge, Clayton Varley, and Grace Hahn—three of the best English majors at Missouri Baptist University—for their reader response essays on this volume. I also appreciate Rebecca (Reba) Duke, an MBU colleague, who kindly sent me words of praise for the back cover, and to Mary Ellen Fuquay, Mason Arledge, and Grace Hahn for their editorial advice. It is a delight to note that the following chapters in this book developed out of prior publications:

- "Haiku Pilgrimage to Tokyo, Japan: Photos and Haiku" (11 poems). *Cantos: A Literary and Arts Journal* 24 (2018), pp. 67-73.

- "A Short Life, a Big Presence: Higuchi Sites in Tokyo." *Cantos* 25 (2019), pp. 95-101.

- "Natsume Soseki Sites at or Near the University of Tokyo: A Photo Essay." *The Right Words* 8 (May 2019), pp. 36-43.

- "Shiki and Soseki Sites in Matsuyama, the 'Haiku Capital': A Photo Essay." *The Right Words: A Magazine of Nonfiction* 9 (Dec. 2019), pp. 28-40.

- "Onomichi, Fumiko Hayashi's Home during Her Early Years: A Photo Essay." *The Right Words* 9 (Dec. 2019), pp. 46-55.

- "In Search of Kawabata's Dancer: The Izu Peninsula: A Photo Essay." *The Right Words* 10 (Mar. 2020), pp. 35-45.

- "Gems of Japanese Literature: The Path of Literature in Onomichi: A Photo Essay." *The Right Words* 10 (Mar. 2020), pp. 38-47.

Finally, the title of this book, "On the Road Again," comes from the second paragraph of Matsuo Basho's (1644-94) famous travelogue *The Narrow Road to the Deep North*:

> It was only towards the end of last autumn that I returned from rambling along the coast. I barely had time to sweep the cobwebs from my broken house on the River Sumida before the New Year, but no sooner had the spring mist begun to rise over the field than I wanted to be on the road again to cross the barrier-gate of Shirakawa [in Fukushima Prefecture] in due time.
>
> (*The Narrow Road to the Deep North and Other Travel Sketches*. Trans. Nobuyuki Yuasa. New York: Penguin, 1966, p. 97)

As a poet consumed by wanderlust, the haiku master "could not stay idle at home" (p. 97). In 1689, he left Edo (Tokyo), starting a long journey to northeastern Japan in search of poetic inspiration. Upon returning home, he wrote the *Narrow Road*, which adopts the form of haibun (haiku writing). While making my own literary pilgrimages in Japan for more than a decade, I roamed under the spell of the same desire to see the sites connected with famous writers and poets.

Foreword
By
C. Clark Triplett, Ph.D.

Travelogues have a long and distinguished literary history starting as early as the ancient Greek historian Herodotus whose *Histories* (425 B.C.) details the Greco-Persian wars. In spite of the many fanciful and mythical digressions that stretch the imagination, his work provides a wealth of information about the cultural and ethnographic landscape of the time. Since that early work, some of the most celebrated writers have contributed to this genre of literature, including Marco Polo (*The Travels of Marco Polo*), Mark Twain (*The Innocents*), Jack Kerouac (*On the Road*), and Laurence Sterne (*A Sentimental Journey through France and Italy*), to name a few. More recently authors such as Anthony Bourdain (*World Travel: An Irreverent Guide*) and William Least Heat-Moon (*Blue Highways*), have penned wildly popular books that explore nature, obscure locations, and exotic foods. The list of interesting and worthwhile books is extensive and covers a range of topics that consider not only exotic locations, but also uncomfortable and nitty-gritty experience of life in third-world prisons (Rusty Young's *Marching Powder*). Most of the good ones inevitably change the world of the reader and transform the way readers see themselves in the context of these sometimes strange and curious landscapes that some would never experience apart from the writer's unique journey. In some cases, the narrative assists the reader in facing lifelong fears and in finding the courage to chase new dreams of adventure and beauty.

John Han's *On the Road Again* is a photographic and narrative exploration of the sites of legendary Japanese writers and poets including Basho, Higuchi, Soseki, Fumiko, Mishima, and Kawabata. It is a work in the best tradition of travel books with the addition of multiple illustrative photographs of historic locations and representations of personal artifacts of these well-known and storied writers. Interestingly, some of the writers represented in this volume were "consumed with wanderlust" and traveled frequently to find inspiration for their work. Han himself is no stranger to literary pilgrimages around the United States and throughout East Asia. He is a resident of two worlds and his extensive writing chronicles the common life of the land of his birth in South Korea and his current home in the United States. For more than a decade, he has annually participated in the scholarly meetings of the John Steinbeck Society of Japan, presenting papers and leading conferences on literature and poetry writing. Han's own heritage, a mixture of Korean and Japanese cultures, and his acute interest in world literature and Japanese verse give him a unique perspective on the life and journeys of these legendary Japanese poets and writers.

In this delightful excursion deep into Japanese culture and literary history, Han leads the reader from quaint little villages, obscure coastal cities, and forgotten locations to a wealth of historical background and literary memorabilia that will gratify both the prosaic traveler as well as the gifted lyricist. The author's travel story is a blending of history, biography, and travelogue that offers a unique combination of insights, notable quotations, and arcane artifacts that will pique the interest of most avid explorers of Japanese culture. This work will also inspire readers to scratch deeper into a different world that often seems inscrutable to many Western observers.

On the Road is both a personal story and a journey into the lives and products of the great Japanese masters. Han encourages the reader to join the expedition as way of introducing the consumer to the unfamiliar but alluring nature of Japanese culture and the beauty of ancient oriental verse. Having written numerous articles and books on haiku and senryu, among other forms of Asian poetry, Han guides the reader to notable historical sites to explore the origins of the best of Japanese literature. Through photography, poetry, and historical events, Han paints a captivating picture of the life of the poet that the reader will find beguiling and memorable. The work will also appeal to the more thoughtful reader who is not only interested in the historical *sitz im leben* (setting in life) of Japanese poetry, but the mechanisms and inception of the best of Asian verse. Interestingly, Han uses the occasion of his visits to various sites as an opportunity to compose his own verses as a reflection on the spirit of writers like Basho:

> Basho shrine
> At the traveler's approach
> Flags flutter

> or

> Basho haiku path
> Strolling down the alley
> Amid the city din

These verses provide a context and poetic imagery for understanding the intellectual and emotional journey of both the author and the ancient master. Han's description of what may seem to the reader a mundane event or experience in the life of the poet provides a means for gaining an intuitive understanding of the nature of human experience and the implicit beauty of everyday life. Although the contemplative life of a Japanese poet may seem alien to many Westerners, it portrays an everyday world that matters from a perspective that the reader may have never experienced. Han teases out the idea of much of Japanese lyrics that there may be lustrous gems even in the most banal events and experiences. The greatest writers seem to have the ability to reveal deep and vibrant truths and lessons of life even in the most humdrum of circumstances.

Interested readers will find Han's *On the Road Again* a journey worth pursuing. At the end of the journey, readers may discover an emotional part of themselves they never realized was there. The odyssey of the author and the Japanese masters reflects a drive to seek out and discover the unknown as well as novel and unusual perspectives on nature and the common life. While there is much to gain both intellectually and emotionally from this work, perhaps, more importantly, it will challenge the reader to step outside of her comfort zone as means to grow as a human being.

C. Clark Triplett (Ph.D., St. Louis University) is Emeritus Dean of Graduate Studies and Professor of Psychology at Missouri Baptist University. He served as co-editor (with John Han) of *The Final Crossing: Death and Dying in Literature* (New York: Peter Lang, 2015) and as co-editor (with John Han and Ashley Anthony) of *Worlds Gone Awry: Essays on Dystopian Fiction* (Jefferson, NC: McFarland, 2018). Triplett is the author of many articles and book reviews published in *Intégrité* and *Cantos*, and his haiku have appeared in the *Asahi Haikuist Network* (Japan), *Cantos*, and *Fireflies' Light*. A native of St. Louis, he earned a B.A. from Southwest Baptist University, an M.Div. from Covenant Theological Seminary, an M.S.Ed. from Southern Illinois University at Edwardsville, and a Ph.D. from Saint Louis University.

Introductory Notes

The Genesis of This Book

Since 2007, I have had the pleasure of visiting Japan to attend the annual John Steinbeck conference every year except for one. Organized by the John Steinbeck Society of Japan, the conference meets in Tokyo and other cities—such as Hiroshima, Kyoto, Sapporo, Shizuoka, and Naha—in alternate years. Before or after the annual meeting, I typically spend a day or two for literary tourism before flying to South Korea, where my mother and siblings live. Similar to China and South Korea, Japan cherishes its own cultural heritage, preserving literary sites across the country. Statues of famous writers and poets stand in public places, their former residences are open to the public, and numerus tanka and haiku rocks dot the land. It is hard not to notice that Japanese society holds literary art in high esteem. The preponderance of literary destinations also reflects Japan's unique approach to modernity: the pursuit of science and technology without undermining its own cultural traditions.

As a poet particularly interested in Japanese verse forms, I had long wished to visit locations connected to haiku masters—such as Matsuo Basho (1644-94), Yosa Buson (1716-84), Kobayashi Issa (I763-1827), and Masaoka Shiki (1867-1902)—and other literary giants. Finally, in 2007, I began to explore some of those sites. Although the conference locations and my tight schedules prevented me from making systematic trip plans, I still had the pleasure of seeing with my own eyes important haiku sites, as well as locations related to other literary types. Every site I visited filled me with an overwhelming sense of awe, and I took hundreds of photos. During the past couple of years, I have published seven photo essays on some of the locations in *Cantos: A Literary and Arts Journal* and *The Right Words: A Magazine of Nonfiction*. Along with three new photo essays, they are now republished in *On the Road Again* for those who have a fondness for Japanese writing. It is my hope that this book will motivate my readers to visit Japan and see the sights in person.

Musings on Korea and Japan: Personal and Historical Connections

As a native of South Korea, I have always found Japan fascinating for personal and historical reasons. Two years ago, my DNA test—conducted by National Geographic—revealed that I was genetically more Japanese than Korean. Maybe this explains why I feel comfortable during my visits to Japan. The test results were somewhat surprising but not completely. Indeed, the relationship between Korea and Japan spans more than 2,000 years.[1] The interactions between Baekje (13 B.C.-660 A.D.)—the ancient kingdom located in my native province—and Japan were particularly active. In 538 A.D., Japan received Buddhism via Baekje, and Baekje immigrants to Japan carried with them rice cultivation, wheel-thrown pottery, systems of social ranking, law codes and government, and the classic texts of Confucius.[2] When Baekje lost to the united forces of Silla from southeastern Korea and the Tang Dynasty in 660, more than 200,000 people fled to Japan. Whenever I visit Kyoto and Hiroshima in western Japan, I envision the presence of Korean blood in many of the Japanese people walking on the street. Indeed, during his 68th birthday press conference, Japanese emperor Akihito recognized his imperial ancestry's genetic connection with Korea: "I, on my part, feel a certain kinship with Korea, given the fact that it is recorded in the *Chronicles of Japan* [日本書紀 *The Nihon Shoki*, 720] that the mother of Emperor Kammu [r. 781-806] was of the line of King Muryong of Paekche [r. 501-523]"[3] Although some Japanese do not seem excited about the imperial house's Korea connection, it is historically proven that Chinese, Koreans, and Japanese have interconnected with each other for thousands of years—as in the case of Britons, Germans, and French.

In ancient and early medieval times, Japan turned to the continent of Asia for an advanced civilization. The tide turned the other way around as Japan modernized itself rapidly after opening its doors to the United States in the mid-nineteenth century. By 1900, Japan became a major power in the world, and Chinese and Koreans began to turn to Japan for Western learning. Japanese considered their country the vehicle for transmitting Western civilization to the rest of Asia, the supposedly inferior nations; Japan was part of Asia geographically but outside Asia culturally. The idea that Japan was destined to save the rest of Asia sounds like an Oriental version of Manifest Destiny. Kanzo Uchimura (1861-1930), a Christian evangelist in Japan, embraced it. In his book on Kanzo,[4] Hiroshi Miura discusses Kanzo's idea as follows:

> A country's geographical location (as well as its race) shows that country's mission. Japan, as a gateway to Asia, was charged with a great mission that could unite one half of the world with the other half. Only by going through Japan can China, Korea, India, Persia, and Turkey be saved. Thus, the destiny of more than half of the human race rested on Japan's shoulders. Japan was not created to satisfy the avarice of a few indolent peers and greedy merchants. Japan's reason for existence was to save over 400 million Chinese, over 250 million Indians, and thousands of millions of others on the Asiatic continent. The hope of Japan inheres in its mission. (62-63)

A sense of sacred mission evident in this passage reflects the ways in which many Japanese in the Meiji, Taishō, and Shōwa eras thought: Western civilization was superior, and Japan had the moral obligation to spread it among its inferior Asian neighbors. The intention to share the benefits of Western civilization was good, but history tells us how the idea of a chosen people can be destructive as well.

In Korea, there are endless debates about whether Japanese colonialism was instrumental to the modernization of Korea. My personal view is that it was, even if Japan modernized Korea to exploit its resources. During the years of my employment at Si-sa-yong-o-sa Publishers in Seoul (1981-87), I learned firsthand the important role Japan played in disseminating Western culture and modern technology. In the area of publishing, the Japanese industry was a model for Korean companies. We copied ideas, trends, and even products from the Japanese publishing companies without giving credit—by using Japan's thirty-six-year-long (1910-45) colonial rule of Korea as a pretext. For instance, as soon as a Japanese firm translated an English novel into Japanese, a Korean publisher hired someone who knew Japanese so that he could translate the Japanese version into Korean; the company advertised its "Korean translation" of the English-language novel without acknowledging that the original text was in Japanese, not in English. For the Koreans who know Japanese (including those who lived under Japanese colonial rule), translating Japanese into Korean is relatively easy: the two languages have the same word order, and almost all of the content words in the two languages use the same Chinese characters anyway. By the time I left Korea for the United States in 1988, Si-sa-yong-o-sa had begun to buy copyrights from American and Japanese companies and pay royalties; other publishing firms in Korea followed suit as well. Korea's economy was growing fast, so it was time to stop pirating.

Anyone who has basic knowledge of East Asian history knows the thorny events that soured the relationship among China, Korea, and Japan in the twentieth century. During the last two decades, however, the power dynamics among the three countries have changed significantly. China has replaced Japan as a G2 country, and its military is the third strongest in the world. South Korea's economy is the eleventh largest and its military the seventh strongest. Japan is a G3 country, and its military is the sixth strongest. Despite their rivalries and suspicions toward each other, the three countries should make continued efforts to live for mutual survival and prosperity. One of the best ways to maintain international peace is to learn about each other's cultural heritage. Because China, Korea, and Japan belong to the Confucian cultural sphere, it is easy for their citizens to relate to each other through cultural exchanges. Reading literature and visiting well-known literary sites can be a starting point. Koreans who criticize their compatriots for liking Japanese culture should read Japanese texts and visit some of the literary destinations featured in *On the Road Again*. They will find those texts and sites highly moving and relatable.

As a naturalized citizen living in the American Midwest, I sometimes feel foreign because the majority of the people have a different skin color. Strangers remind me of my immigrant background by asking the seemingly innocuous yet offensive question "Where are you originally from?" During my visits to Japan, however, I can easily blend in with the locals, who assume that I am one of them until they find out that I do not speak their language. I comprehend roughly eighty percent of written Japanese, so it is not difficult to travel alone in Japan. After visiting many literary landmarks in Japan, I have learned that literature is one of the best ways to understand and connect with people of another country. In spite of their differences, human beings have common emotions and life struggles. My travels in Japan have also brought me into contact with many kind people, who helped me when I was lost. They were not demons some Koreans consider them to be. Reading this book will certainly allow them to become more empathetic toward Japan and Japanese people. Happy reading!

Notes

[1] Some scholars believe that the original settlers of Japan came from three neighboring regions: Sakhalin, the Korean Peninsula, and Taiwan. Meanwhile, *Nippon: The Land and Its People* describes the origin of the Japanese people as follows: "[Aborigines] are themselves are the true ancestors of the present Japanese people. Later, when large numbers of people began migrating to Japan from China, Korea and Southeast Asia, they and their cultures were gradually absorbed by the earlier settlers" (33). Regardless of who the "true ancestors" are, it is clear that many Korean immigrants became ancestors of the present-day Japanese. For more information, see *Nippon: The Land and Its People* (Tokyo: Gakuseisha Publishing, 1982).

[2] See Mark Cartwright's article "Ancient Korean & Japanese Relations" at www.ancient.eu/article/982/ancient-korean--japanese-relations/.

[3] For more information, see the article "The Emperor's New Roots" at www.theguardian.com/world/2001/dec/28/japan.worlddispatch. "Paekche" is another way to spell "Baekje."

[4] For more information, see Hiroshi Miura's *The Life and Thought of Kanzo Uchimura, 1861-1930* (Eerdmans, 1996).

Note on the Front Cover Photo

The front-cover photo of this book shows the haiku poet Masaoka Shiki (1867-1902) writing his death poems (*jisei*) and three people on hand reverently observing him; the setting is his hermitage (*Shiki-an*) in Tokyo. The replica is on display in the Shiki Memorial Museum, Matsuyama City, Japan. Taken in May 2012, the photo below shows the small backyard outside his sickroom.

Note on the Back Cover Photo

I took the selfie on the back cover during my visit to Tokyo in 2012. The background shows a small artificial pond at Basho Memorial Museum Annex along the Sumida River. An old pond appears in Matsuo Basho's well-known haiku—perhaps the most famous haiku in history:

> old pond
> a frog jumps into
> the sound of water
>   (trans. Jane Reichhold)

Upon returning to my hotel room, I scribbled five haiku:

> new pond
> goldfish make
> no sound

> new pond
> goldfish's endless search
> for Basho

new pond
silent sound the tails
of goldfish make

new pond
too shallow for a frog
to dive into

new pond
goldfish pause to listen
to the Sumida

Haiku Pilgrimage to Tokyo

A view of Tokyo in which tradition and modernity co-exist.
Photo by John J. Han.

Once a swamp, Tokyo is one of the largest cities in the world; the population stands at 13.6 million. Kyoto was the political and cultural center of the nation for approximately 1,000 years. Edo (present-day Tokyo) became the capital in 1603, when Shogun Tokugawa Ieyasu established it as his headquarters. In 1868, the emperor's residence moved from Kyoto to Edo, whose name changed to Tokyo the following year. In addition to the nation's capital, Tokyo is the nation's cultural center that attracts artists from all over the nation. Accordingly, it is not surprising that there are many sites and monuments related to haiku. Below are twelve photos and my accompanying haiku. Most of the places are located along the Sumida River (隅田川 *Sumida-gawa*), which flows north to south in central Tokyo.

Photos 1-8: Matsuo Basho Sites along the Sumida River, Tokyo:

The Sumida River frequently appears in Japanese haiku. Kobayashi Issa composed more than fifty haiku set in the river, including the following:

> watching the whiteness
> of summer kimonos...
> Sumida River
> > (trans. David G. Lanoue)

> cats' love calls
> between them flows
> Sumida River
> > (trans. David G. Lanoue)

In his first journal, *The Records of a Weather-Exposed Skeleton*,[1] Matsuo Basho explains why he has decided to leave his hermitage along the Sumida River for a pilgrimage outside Edo (today's Tokyo):

> Following the example of the ancient priest[2] who is said to have travelled thousands of miles caring naught for his provisions and attaining the state of sheer ecstasy under the pure beams of the moon, I left my broken house on the River Sumida in the August of the first year of Jyōkyō among the wails of the autumn wind. (p. 51)

Later, in *The Narrow Road to the Deep North*,[3] his more widely known travelogue, Basho explains how he, stricken with wanderlust again, decided to leave his hut by the Sumida River:

> It was only towards the end of last autumn that I returned from rambling along the coast. I barely had time to sweep the cobwebs from my broken house on the River Sumida before the New Year, but no sooner had the spring mist begun to rise over the field than I wanted to be on the road again to cross the barrier-gate of Shirakawa in due time. (p. 97)

Photos 1-8 were taken at or near Basho Memorial Hall (1-6-3 Tokiwa, Koto-ku, Tokyo). The Hall's website is in Japanese: www.kcf.or.jp/basho/. After taking the photos, I composed the following seven haiku that correspond to the respective photos:

> 1
> Sumida River
> Basho's statue gazes
> at flowing water

2
Basho pond
a few goldfish swim
making no sound

3
stone Basho
he watches a butterfly dance
without motion

4
Basho paperboard
with my face in the hole,
I say *chee-zu*

5
Basho shrine
at the traveler's approach
flags flutter

6-7
a long pilgrimage
to Basho's hut
a fake front

8
Basho haiku path
strolling down the alley
amid the city din

Photo 9: Statue of Matsuo Basho, Arakawa-ku, Tokyo

The statue of Basho stands approximately 8.7 km (5.4 miles) north of Basho Memorial Hall and immediately west of Minami-Senju Station (南千住駅 *Minami-Senju-eki*, "South Senju Station"). Walking for ten minutes to the east will take one to the Sumida River, which flows to southern Tokyo, eventually to Tokyo Bay. The statue turns toward the north—the direction Basho was facing on his trip to the interior in the seventeenth century. At the beginning of *The Narrow Road to the Deep North*, Basho expresses mixed emotions as he says farewell to his friends at Senju: he is happy to be on the road again, yet leaving them behind breaks his heart:

> The faint shadow of Mount Fuji and the cherry blossoms of Ueno and Yanaka were bidding me a last farewell. My friends had got together the night before, and they all came with me on the boat to keep me company for the first few miles. When we got off the boat at Senju, however, the thought of the three thousand miles before me suddenly filled my heart, and neither the houses of the town nor the faces of my friends could be seen by my tearful eyes except as a vision.

> The passing spring,
> Birds mourn,
> Fishes weep
> With tearful eyes.

With this poem to commemorate my departure, I walked forth on my journey, but lingering thoughts made my steps heavy. My friends stood in a line and waved good-bye as long as they could see my back. (pp. 98-99)

Visualizing the moment of Basho's tearful farewell inspired me to compose the following haiku:

> facing north...
> Basho leaves behind
> sounds of car horns

Photos 10-11: Hermitage of Masaoka Shiki in the Neighborhood of Negishi near Uguisudani Station, Tokyo

Although he died at the young age of thirty-five, Masaoka Shiki (1867-1902) is considered an important figure in the development of Japanese poetry. He coined the word *haiku* (俳句), which had been called *hokku*.[4] An innovator of the tanka and haiku forms, he was fond of baseball, which was new to Japan in his time; some of his tanka and haiku deal with baseball. A frequent visitor to Shiki's small hermitage was Natsume Soseki (夏目 漱石, 1867-1916), one of the most important modern novelists in Japan. After visiting Shiki's hermitage and his tombstone, I penned the following two haiku:

> Shiki home
> the small yard filled
> with sunlight

> Shiki's tomb
> a drizzle moistens his name
> little by little

Photo 12: Museum of Haiku Literature

Located in the Shinjuku area of Tokyo, the Museum of Haiku Literature provides resources on the international haiku movement. Its holdings include numerous English-language haiku books and magazines. The website of the Shinjuku Convention and Visitors Bureau provides the following information:

> [The] Museum of Haiku Literature is run by [the] Haiku Literature [A]ssociation, and [is] the only place that has a library that specializes in Haiku Literature. The number of books they keep as of December 2002 amounts to 45,785 Haiku Literature collections, and 269,049 Haiku Literature magazines.
>
> [The] Haiku Literature [A]ssociation issues a bulletin "Museum of Haiku Literature" every month. They aim for the creative development and the spread of Haiku Literature, which in turn contribute to the progress of Japanese culture. To this end, they hold Haiku Literature contests and various seminars, issue bulletins, and interact with foreign countries.[5]

When I arrived at the museum via subway and taxi, several haiku groups were meeting in different rooms. Browsing a catalogue of resources in the museum, I wrote the following haiku:

> haiku museum…
> curious if it holds
> my books

For those who are curious, I did not find any of my books in the museum. My impression was that the museum would be happy to receive donated copies but did not seem to have enough space for too many books anyway. It was a pleasure to see many issues of English haiku journals from the United States, such as *Frogpond* and *Modern Haiku*.

Notes:

[1] Included in Matsuo Bashō, *The Narrow Road to the Deep North and Other Travel Sketches*. Trans. Nobuyuki Yuasa. Penguin, 1966.

[2] Kuang-wên, a Chinese priest of the Nansung dynasty (1127-1279). —Translator's note.

[3] Included in Matsuo Bashō, *The Narrow Road to the Deep North and Other Travel Sketches*. Trans. Nobuyuki Yuasa. Penguin, 1966.

[4] The "starting verse" of an aristocratic collaborative linked poem, *renga*, or of its popular offshoot, *renku* (*haikai no renga*).

[5] www.kanko-shinjuku.jp.e.xm.hp.transer.com/spot/-/article_365.html.

1

2

3

4

5

6-7

8

9

10

11

12

A Short Life, a Big Presence: Ichiyo Higuchi Sites in Tokyo

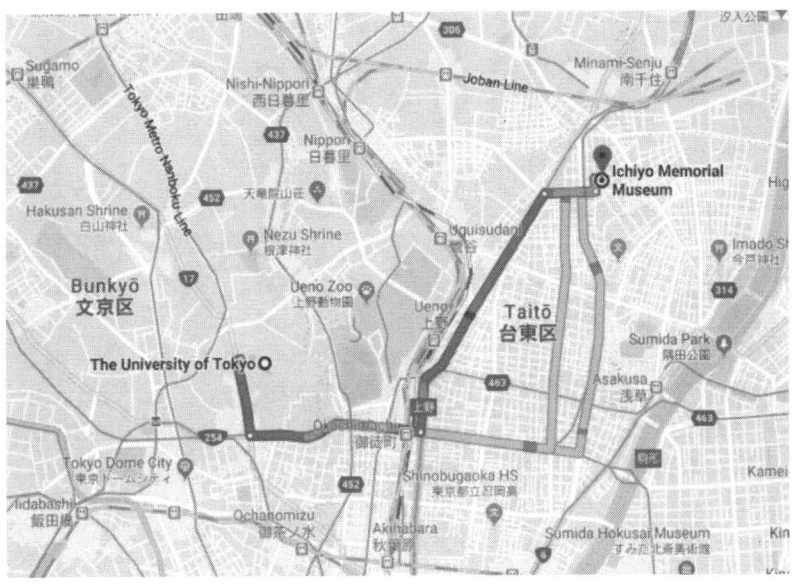

The Ichiyo Memorial Museum is located in Taito Ward approximately three miles northeast of the University of Tokyo, which belongs to Bunkyo Ward. At Minami-Senju, located ¾ miles northeast of the Museum, stands a statue of the haiku poet Matsuo Basho. Courtesy of Google Maps.

Ichiyo Higuchi (樋口 一葉, 1872-1896) is an intriguing writer in the history of modern Japanese fiction. In her short lifetime, she wrote fiction for only four years, but her stories elicit much attention from both scholars and the general populace. She came from a peasant family that had moved to Tokyo, where she was born. When she was seventeen, her father died, leaving his family in a state of destitution. She barely supported her mother and younger sister by doing menial work, such as washing and needlework. Ichiyo became a literary sensation with the publication of her novella *Child's Play* (1895 and 1896). Her characters and events in her fiction are relatable to many readers—poor people who try to survive in a big city, who find solace in friendships, and who help each other.

The short story "Separate Ways," a popularly assigned text in world literature classes in the United States, exemplifies Ichiyo's preoccupation with the life of low-class urbanites in her time. The main characters are Okyō, a seamstress in her early twenties, and Kichizō, a sixteen-year-old apprentice in an umbrella factory. Derided by people for his short stature, Kichizō often visits Okyō, who cares for him as if he were her brother. One day, he hears the rumor that she will leave the area to become someone's mistress. Feeling both abandoned and outraged that she is compromising her virtue, he comes to her to protest. The story ends this way:

> [Kichizō] went to the front door and began to put his sandals on.
> "Kichizō! You're wrong. I'm leaving here, but I'm not abandoning you. You're like my little brother. How can you turn on me?" From behind, she hugged him with all her might. "You're too impatient. You jump to conclusions."
> "You mean you're not going to be someone's mistress?" Kichizō turned around.
> "It's not the sort of thing anybody wants to do. But it's been decided. You can't change things."

He stared at her with tears in his eyes.
"Take your hand off me, Okyō."
(trans. Robert Lyons Danly)

The naturalistic ending of the story makes the reader wonder if she was under the influence of European and American fiction in her time. In fact, she knew little about Western literature. Her literary training was limited to classical Japanese poetry, which she learned by attending the Haginoya (a well-known tanka school run by Utako Nakajima), and to fiction writing, which she learned under the mentorship of Nakarai Tōsui.

On the next few pages, readers will see some of the photos related to Ichiyo Higuchi. I took them on May 19, 2018, during my visit to Tokyo. Below are the details:

1. Considering the author's short lifespan (1872-96), the Ichiyo Memorial Museum in Taito Ward, Tokyo, is very large. This shows the popularity of her works among Japanese today. Ichiyo is a family name, which, in East Asia, precedes a given name.

2. The monument to Ichiyo's short novel *Takekurabe* ("Growing Up," たけくらべ, 1895-96) stands in the Ichiyo Memorial Park. The story is set in Yoshiwara (吉原), the chief licensed pleasure quarter in northeastern Edo (Tokyo). Alongside the short story "Jūsan'ya" ("The Thirteenth Night," 十三夜), *Takekurabe* is considered her best work.

3. The museum displays Ichiyo's complete works, including her stories and diary entries.

4. At the age of seventeen, Ichiyo lost her father and became the sole supporter of her mother and her younger sister. The drawing shows the shabby rented house they inhabited from 1890-93. Slightly taller than the others, it is second from the left, and the author ran the stationary store on the first floor. The

store was in a poor neighborhood, only a five-minute walk from Yoshiwara.

5. The statue of Ichiyo at Hoshinji, a Buddhist temple 200 feet west of the Red Gate of the University of Tokyo, Bunkyo Ward. She lived on the second floor of the building next to the temple.

6. The statue of Ichiyo at Hoshinji (close-up).

7. Google Maps shows the locations of Hoshinji (200 feet west of the University of Tokyo's Red Gate, 東大赤門前) and of the Former Iseya Pawn Shop (舊伊勢屋質店), Bunkyo Ward, Tokyo.

8. Hoshinji also houses the statue of a country girl in fashionable clothing. According to the head priest at the temple, some young women who dressed stylishly used to flock to the University of Tokyo area, strolling in an effort to attract attention from a male student. The University, the most prestigious institution of higher learning in Japan, has produced many of the leading figures in politics and business. A degree from the University is often considered the ticket to success in Japanese society.

9. University of Tokyo students perform a traditional dance at a spring festival before the University's Red Gate (Akamon), May 2018.

10. Old Iseya pawnshop Ichiyo frequented. When a financial emergency arose, she rushed to this wooden shop to borrow money. Located a few blocks west of Hoshinji, the building draws many Ichiyo aficionados on a daily basis. It is registered as a cultural heritage site.

11. The entrance to the pawnshop displays a Chinese-language sign that reads, "Currently Open."

1

2

3

4

5

6

7

8

9

10

11

Natsume Soseki Sites at or near the University of Tokyo

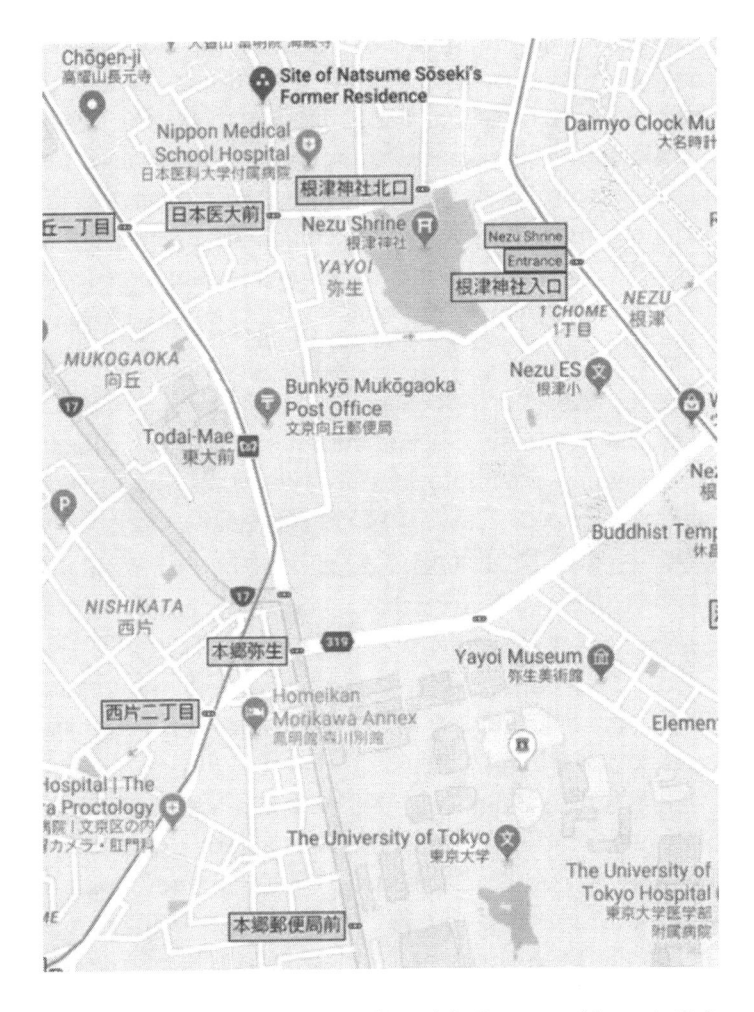

Google Maps shows the location of Soseki's former residence in Tokyo. It is approximately 0.75 mile north of the University of Tokyo.

Natsume Soseki (夏目漱石, 1867-1916) is a towering figure in the history of the modern Japanese novel. The fact that his portrait appeared on Japan's 1000¥ (approximately US$10) banknote in 1984-2004 testifies to his fame. Soseki's fiction piqued my interest in 2013, when I was writing a review of the English translation of his novel *Kokoro* (こころ, 1914; trans. Meredith McKinney, Penguin, 2010). This sad story deals with the triangular relationship among two male friends, Sensei and K, and their landlady's beautiful daughter named Ojosan. Years ago, K took his own life so that Ojosan could marry Sensei. After getting married to Ojosan, Sensei visits the Zoshigaya cemetery every month mourning K's death, but Ojosan does not know exactly what led to K's suicide. *Kokoro* is an intensely sad story, which is typical of many traditional Japanese novels and plays.

    Recently, I also read Soseki's *Sanshirō* (三四郎, 1908), a light-hearted story that focuses on the title character's self-discovery, his academic life, and the cultural differences between his hometown, Kumamoto, and Tokyo, where he attends the University of Tokyo. I have yet to read Soseki's supposedly best work, *I Am a Cat* (吾輩は猫である, *Wagahai wa Neko de Aru*, 1905-06), a picaresque novel that an American professor at Chuo University in Tokyo strongly recommended to me. The main theme of this long novel—Japan's obsessive replication of Western culture during the Meiji era (1868-1912)—appears in *Kokoro* and *Sanshiro* as well.

    All of the Soseki novels mentioned above are set in Tokyo, so it is worth visiting the places in the capital city related to the author, especially the University of Tokyo and his former residence near the campus. On my first visit to the campus in 2007, I knew little about Soseki; at that time, my desire was simply to take some pictures of the University, which is one of the most prestigious institutions of higher learning in Asia. When I visited the campus and the surrounding area for the second time in May 2018, I knew exactly what I wanted to see beforehand. On the next few pages, readers will see some of the photos I took during my 2007 and 2018 visits to Tokyo.

1. East meets West on the University of Tokyo's main campus as is illustrated by the co-existence of different architectural styles.
2. Sanshirō Pond at the University of Tokyo. The following descriptions appear in Soseki's *Sanshirō* (Trans. Jay Rubin):

[Sanshirō] stared at the surface of the pond. The reflection of many trees seemed to reach the bottom, and down deeper than the trees, the blue sky. No longer was he thinking of streetcars, or Tokyo, or Japan. A sense of something far-off and remote had come to take their place. The feeling lasted but a moment, when loneliness began to spread across its surface like a veil of clouds. The solitude was complete, as if he were sitting alone in Nonomiya's cellar. (p. 22)

*

The University was really big and the buildings were really beautiful. There was a pond in the middle of the campus. [Sanshirō] enjoyed walking around it. (p. 32)

3. A campus map shows the location of Sanshirō Pond, which is a five-minute walk from the Red Gate (Akamon).

4. As Japan's first English literary scholar, Soseki studied at University College London in 1901-03. Upon returning to Japan, he lived in a house at this site for three years. During his residence, he wrote his first novel, *I Am a Cat*, a satirical work on modern Japan. Currently, the Alumni Hall of the Nippon (Japan) Medical College stands in the same location.

5. Erected in 1971 (Shōwa 46), this stone marker stands in the place of Soseki's old residence in Bunkyo Ward, a dozen blocks north of the University of Tokyo. It briefly explains Soseki's life, accomplishments, and the significance of this location.

6. This marker states that Soseki's former residence in Bunkyo Ward is not only the starting point of his literary career but also an important historical site for modern Japanese literature.

7. Copies of the Soseki novels in my personal library:

    - *Bochan*. 1906. Trans. J. Cohn. Penguin, 2013. A highly autobiographical novel, it tells the humorous story of a "young master" (Botchan) who becomes a mathematics teacher in Matsuyama on the island of Shikoku but leaves employment in less than two months.

    - *Kusamakura*. 1906. Trans. Meredith McKinney. Penguin, 2008. Intended as a "haiku-style novel," it follows a nameless artist who—like the haiku poet Matsuo Basho—embarks on a journey of self-discovery.

    - *Sanshirō*. 1908. Trans. J. Rubin. Penguin, 2010. The title character, a new University of Tokyo student from rural Kumamoto, undergoes many incidents that open his eyes to academia, urban lifestyle, Western civilization, and female psychology.

    - *Kokoro*. 1914. Trans. Edwin McClellan.

Regnery Publishing, 1996. In this love triangle story, a young man commits suicide so that his friend can marry the woman they both love.

Each of these books is a uniquely intriguing read, but my favorite is *Kokoro*. My review of the translation by Meredith McKinney (Penguin, 2010) appeared in *Cantos: A Literary and Arts Journal*, Volume 19 (2013), pp. 104-05. Part of the review reads,

> *Kokoro* is a typical Japanese work in that it moves slowly and not much takes place. Similar to many other Japanese novels (Yasunari Kawabata's *Snow Country* and Yukio Mishima's *The Temple of the Golden Pavilion* come to mind), it is filled with sadness and sorrow. In its pensive, contemplative atmosphere, it is contrasted with action-oriented, adventurous Western fiction, such as *Gulliver's Travels*, *Robinson Crusoe*, *Candide*, *Moby-Dick*, *Dracula*, and *The Old Man and the Sea*. Soseki's main character, Sensei, suffers lifelong guilt toward K—his roommate, dear friend, and romantic rival—who commits suicide when Sensei announces that he has obtained permission to marry Ojosan, the woman both men love. A depressed man preoccupied with death and dying, Sensei also kills himself although he is not entirely responsible for K's suicide.
>
> By falling in love with the woman Sensei loves, K may not win the applause from readers at first. However, near the end of the novel, he powerfully elicits sympathy. Both men are drawn to the same woman as if by destiny, their friendship turns sour, and an act of suicide ends their triangular relationship. Ironically, Ojosan does not know why

the two men died in succession and what they really felt about her. In his suicide note, K does not mention Ojosan to prevent Sensei from being implicated. Sensei, who eventually marries Ojosan, does not tell her why K committed suicide and why he himself follows suit: because he loves her dearly, he does not want to soil her purity and innocence.

Meanwhile, my double Fibonacci poem inspired by *Kokoro* appeared in Issue #2 (Nov. 2012) of *Fireflies' Light: A Chapbook of Short Poems*:

His Unspoken Words

"It would seem that K received his final blow with great composure."
—Natsume Soseki, *Kokoro* (1914)

It's
hard,
so hard
to erase
you out of my heart
which you have occupied so long.

It's not that hard to let you go.
The hard question is,
why did I
linger
so

1

2

3

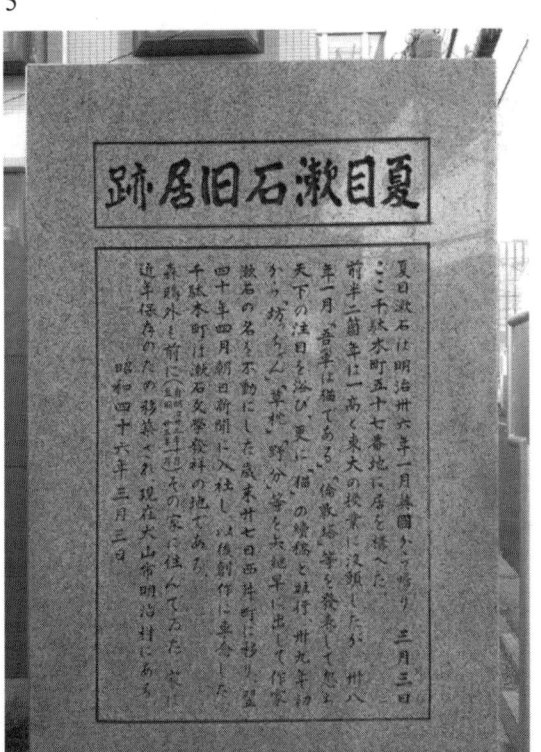

4

5

夏目漱石旧居跡

夏目漱石は明治卅六年一月英国より帰り三月三日ここ千駄木町五十七番地に居を構えた。前半二箇年は一高と東大の授業に没頭したが卅八年一月「吾輩は猫である」「倫敦塔」等を発表して忽ち天下の注目を浴び、更に「猫」の続篇と妹分「坊ちゃん」「草枕」「野分」等を此処で出て作家漱石の名を不動にした歳末廿七日西片町に移り翌四十年四月朝日新聞に入社し以後創作に専念した千駄木町は漱石文学発祥の地であり森鴎外を前に(観潮楼跡記念碑)ここに住んでおられたが近年係争のため移築され現在犬山市明治村にある

昭和四十六年三月三日

6

夏目漱石旧居跡（区指定史跡）

日本医科大学同窓会館　文京区向丘2-20-7

夏目漱石　本名・金之助。慶応3年〜大正5年(1867〜1916)。小説家。この地に、漱石がイギリス留学から帰国後の、明治36年3月から39年12月、現在の西片1丁目に移るまで、3年10か月住んだ家があった。（家主は東大同期の斉藤阿具氏）

当時、東京帝大英文科、第一高等学校講師として教職にあった漱石は、この地で初めて創作の筆をとった。その作品『吾輩は猫である』の舞台として、"猫の家"と呼ばれ親しまれた。

この地で、『倫敦塔』『坊っちゃん』『草枕』などの名作を次々に発表し、一躍文壇に名をあらわした。漱石文学発祥の地である。

漱石が住む13年程前の明治23年10月から1年余り森鷗外が住み、文学活動に励んだ。鷗外は、ここから団子坂上の観潮楼へ移っていった。

二大文豪の居住の地、漱石文学発祥の地として、近代文学史上の重要な史跡である。旧居は、愛知県犬山市の「明治村」に移築保存してある。

―郷土愛をはぐくむ文化財―

文京区教育委員会　　平成7年3月

7

Peace and Tranquility: Literary Treasures in Kyoto

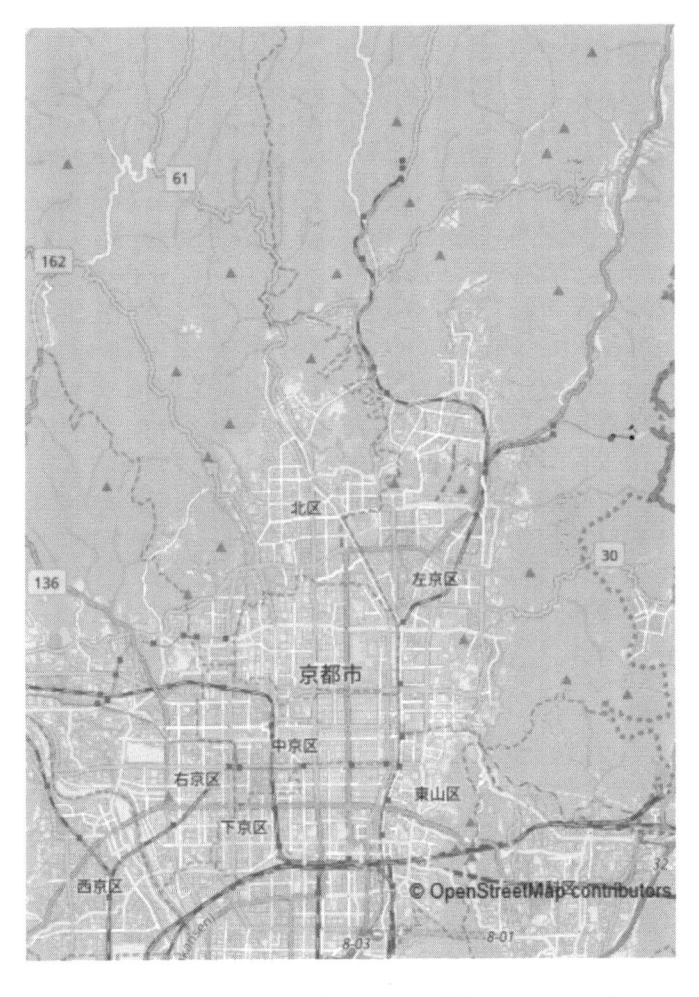

The map shows most of the areas of Kyoto—central, eastern, western, and northern.
Map source: "© OpenStreetMap contributors"

Kyoto (literally "Capital City") was the capital of Japan from 794 until 1868, when Tokyo replaced it as Japan's new seat of government. Its nicknames include Heian-kyo ("Capital of Peace and Tranquility"), Miyako ("The Capital"), Saikyo ("Western Capital"), and Sennen no Miyako ("Thousand-Year Capital"). As the nation's capital for more than 1,000 years, it served as the political and cultural center through classical, medieval, and early modern periods: Heian (7941185), Kamakura (11851333), Muromachi (13331568), AzuchiMomoyama (15681600), and Edo (16001868). Unsurprisingly, Kyoto is home to seventeen UNESCO World Heritage Sites. Indeed, visiting Kyoto—the site of an ancient imperial palace as well as thousands of Buddhist temples and Shinto shrines—is like entering the distant past of the nation itself. Even during the Pacific War, the United States spared Kyoto from bombings. Kyoto is also an academic city—the home of dozens of universities, such as the University of Kyoto, Ritsumeikan University, and Doshisha University. Thanks to its historical and cultural importance, the city attracts numerous tourists from all over Japan and the world. In springtime, many schools bring their students to Kyoto on a "learning excursion." Unlike other Japanese cities, it is sometimes hard to find a hotel room unless one makes a reservation in advance.

*

I visited Kyoto—the most historic city in Japan—in 2010 and 2016. Despite my time constraints, I was fortunate enough to visit several literary destinations in the city, including Kinkakuji, Ryoanji, the ancient imperial palace, and Doshisha University. It was great to feel the presence of the ancient past in this peaceful city of 1.5 million people.

Kinkakuji (The Temple of the Golden Pavilion)

Kinkakuji, a Zen Buddhist temple in northwestern Kyoto, is one of the seventeen Historic Monuments of Ancient Kyoto, which are also World Heritage Sites. Its official name is

Rokuonji (鹿苑寺, "Deer Garden Temple"). A twenty-two-year-old acolyte named Hayashi Yoken burnt it down in 1950, but it was rebuilt in 1955. Prior to my first visit, I had seen many photos of the Golden Pavilion and imagined a marvelous sight. When I actually visited the temple, it came across as a beautiful—not an extraordinarily beautiful—one. Yet, the presence of many tourists there made me realize that I was visiting a truly famous site.

Kinkakuji is the setting of Yukio Mishima's (1925-70) well-known novel *The Temple of the Golden Pavilion* (1956), which Ivan Morris translated into English in 1959. The story deals with the destruction of the temple by Mizoguchi, a young priest in training. Mizoguchi's father used to tell him about the perfect beauty of the temple. In Chapter 1, the arsonist-narrator recalls,

> Ever since my childhood, Father had often spoken to me about the Golden Temple.[…] Father had never told me that the real Golden Temple was shining in gold, or anything of the sort; yet, according to Father, there was nothing on this earth so beautiful as the Golden Temple. (*The Temple of the Golden Pavilion*. Trans. Ivan Morris. New York: Berkeley Medallion Books, 1959, pp. 21-22)

An "ugly" youth who stutters, Mizoguchi grows up having difficulty socializing with people: "My stuttering, I need hardly say, placed an obstacle between me and the outside world" (23). A possible reason for his arson is an acute self-awareness of his physical deficiencies: the temple's perfect beauty keeps reminding him of his ugliness and eventually angers him to the point of setting it on fire. Moments before he burns down the Golden Pavilion, he both admires and antagonizes the building as follows:

> The beauty of the Golden Temple was unsurpassed. And

I knew now where my great weariness had come from. That beauty was taking a last chance to exercise its power over me and to bind me with that impotence which has so often overcome me in the past. (p. 279)

Another reason for Mizoguchi's criminal act seems to be his suicidal tendency. After setting the building on fire, he intends to perish along with it, but he flees the scene. The last possible reason is his desire for salvation through a supposedly Zen act: killing whom or what one reveres so that it does not become a hindrance to one's pursuit of enlightenment:

> "Face the back, face the outside, and if ye meet, kill instantly!"
>
> Yes, the first sentence went like that. The famous passage in that chapter of the *Rinsairoku*. Then the remaining words emerged fluently: "When ye meet the Buddha, kill the Buddha! When ye meet your ancestor, kill your ancestor! When ye meet a disciple of Buddha, kill the disciple! When ye meet your father and mother, kill your kin! Only thus will ye attain deliverance. Only thus will ye escape the trammels of material things and become free." (p. 281)

Of course, the sutra does not admonish literal killings for the sake of enlightenment. A young man who is still learning Zen teachings, Mizoguchi misunderstands the passage in the sacred book.

Ryoanji

Similar to Kinkakuji, Ryoanji (龍安寺, "The Temple of the Dragon at Peace") is a Zen Buddhist temple. Like the Golden

Pavilion, it is also one of the seventeen Historic Monuments of Ancient Kyoto (World Heritage Sites). Located 0.87 mile southwest of the Golden Pavilion, it is particularly famous for its *karesansui* (枯山水, "dry landscape") rock garden which represents Buddhist mindfulness and meditation. Unsurprisingly, it is a popular destination for Zen Buddhists, yoga practitioners, and haiku poets.

Ryoanji appears in many Western poems. Tim Reynolds's first commercially published verse collection is entitled *Ryoanji* (New York: Harcourt, Brace, 1964; 58 pages). The book's front cover features a black-and-white photo of the rock garden, and the front flap of the book reads,

> These poems delight the ear and the mind. They rise out of an infinite variety of experience, knowledge, interest, thought and feeling [...] one of the excitements of the book is the suspense with which one watches the poet give shape and unity, beauty and meaning to what may seem, at first, unlikely and oddly assorted materials.

John M. Steadman's *Ryoanji Temple and Other Poems* (Edwin Mellen Press, 1993; 54 pages) is another poetry collection that features the Kyoto temple.

More recently, Leza Lowitz recalls Royanji in her poetry book *Yoga Poems: Lines to Unfold By* (Berkeley, CA: Stone Bridge Press, 2000; 128 pages). The first stanza of the poem "Virasana / Hero" (p. 72) reads,

> I remember Ryoanji—
> how I sat for days at the Kyoto temple,
> stared at the sea of pebbles
> imagining them into shapes
> rocks becoming islands
> a mother tiger and her cubs

ships lost at sea
thoughts in the swirling mind
planets swimming around the sun
then finally just rocks
the rectangle of pebbles
walled in by mud, grass, and clay
a reflecting pool for humanity
and nothing but nothing
answering back
And it didn't matter.
I looked at the lone figure
sitting on the smooth wooden stairs
next to me, and he
looked at me wordlessly,
and understood. (72)

The Sanskrit word *virasana* is a combination of *vira* ("hero") and *asana* ("pose"). It refers to the yoga pose that helps make the legs, knees, and feet more flexible. An American expatriate who writes poems and teaches yoga in Tokyo, Lowitz (b. 1962) portrays the pose as she recalls her visit to Ryoanji.

Doshisha University

Doshisha University (同志社大学, *Doshisha daigaku*) is a prestigious Protestant university founded in 1875. Its founder, Joseph Hardy Neesima (Japanese name: Niijima Jo, 新島 襄, 1843-90), was born in Edo (Tokyo) and was educated at Phillips Academy, Amherst College, and Andover Theological Seminary before returning to Japan as a missionary and educator. The campus is located in the northern part of the city across the street from Kyoto Imperial Palace (京都御所).

In addition to being a high-profile academic institution, Doshisha University is the alma mater of two Korean poets: Yun Dong-ju (1917-1945) and Jeong Ji-yong (1902-ca. 1950). The Christian university honors the two figures from Korea—a former colony—with stone markers. Yoon Dong-ju was born in Jiandao (called Gando among Koreans), Northeast China, where his Korean grandparents had settled in 1886. After completing his studies at Gwangmyeong Secondary School, he entered Yonhi College (present-day Yonsei University) in Seoul in 1938. Upon graduation from Yonhi in 1941, Yun moved to Japan to further his education. After studying English literature at Rikkyo University in Tokyo for six months, he transferred to the College of Humanities at Doshisha University. As a student from Japan's then colony, he was monitored by the National Police Agency, which arrested him for a political offence in 1943. The following year, the Kyoto Regional Courthouse handed him a two-year prison term. He died in the Fukuoka prison on February 16, 1945, at age twenty-seven; he was not fortunate enough to see his motherland liberated from Japan on August 15th that year. His body is buried in his hometown, Jiandao.

A lyric poet, Jeong Ji-yong was born in Okcheon County, North Chungcheong, South Korea. After marrying Song Jae Sook at age eleven, he became a Roman Catholic under his father's influence; the poet's baptismal name was Francis. After finishing Okcheon Public School, he entered Hwimun High School in Seoul. In April 1923, Jeong entered the Department of English at Doshisha University. After earning his bachelor's degree in 1929, he returned to Korea, serving as an English teacher at Huimun High School. In 1945, he became a professor of literature and dean of the College of Arts at Ewha Women's University. When the North Korean Army captured Seoul during the Korean War in 1950, he disappeared while staying in Seoul. Some historians speculate that, as one of dozens of intellectuals the North Korean forces took to the north, he died in a U.S. bombing along the way.

Photo Captions:

1. At the entrance of Kinkakuji stands a rock whose inscription reads,

   World Heritage
   Kinkaku Dear Garden Temple

2. Background information at the entrance of Kinkakuji is in four languages: Japanese, English, Chinese, and Korean. The English version reads,

   Rokuonji Temple (The Temple of the Golden Pavilion)

   Rokuonji Temple is the outer sub-temple of the Shokokuji School of the Rinzai sect of Zen Buddhism. It was registered in UNESCO's World Heritage List in 1994.
   Yoshimitsu Ashikaga, the third shogun of the Muromachi Shogunate Regime, established a villa called Kitayama-den in 1397. After his death, the villa was converted into a Zen temple and was named Rokuonji Temple after Yoshimitsu's posthumous name. Shari-den "Kinkaku (Golden Pavilion)," where the ashes of Sakyamuni, the founder of Buddhism, are supposed to be enshrined, is particularly famous. Thus, the temple is commonly called the Golden Pavilion Temple.

The pavilion is a three-story building. Each floor is built in a different style; the first floor in the court noblemen's residence style of the Heian period, the second floor in the samurai warriors' house style, and the third floor in the Zen temple style. Gold leafing has been applied to the second and third floors over the lacquered surface. On the top of the roof has been placed the brilliant figure of Ho-o, a legendary bird in China. The statues of Yoshimitsu Ashikaga and the crowned Sakyamuni Tathagata on the first floor, the statues of Kannon sitting in the cave and Shitenno (Four Heavenly Kings) on the second floor, and the ashes of Sakyamuni on the third floor are enshrined on their respective floors.

The pavilion was set [on] fire and burned down in 1950. It was restructured in 1955 and lacquer and gold leafing were reapplied in 1987.

The spacious stroll garden with the lake, Kyokochi, has been designated both a Special Historic Site and a Special Scenic Spot by the government. On the north side of Kyokochi, in which the Golden Pavilion is reflected, is located Sekkatei, a tea house famous for its staggered shelves of bush clover and an alcove post made from a nandina tree.

Kyoto City

3. The Golden Pavilion Temple is reflected in the pond of Kyokochi. In *The Temple of the Golden Pavilion,* Mishima describes the beauty of the pond as follows:

When the Golden Temple reflected the evening sun or shone in the moon, it was the light of the water that made the entire structure look as if it were mysteriously floating along and flapping its wings.

The strong bonds of the temple's form were loosened by the reflection of the quivering water, and at such moments the Golden Temple seemed to be constructed of materials like wind and water and flame that are constantly in motion. (p. 279)

4. A close-up photo of the Golden Pavilion Temple. Similar to other historic sites in Japan, the building looks spotless. Indeed, cleanliness is essential part of Japanese culture.

5. By posing before the building and the pond, I wanted to create evidence of my visit to the Golden Pavilion Temple. In this 2010 photo, I look much younger—and somewhat leaner—than I do today. At that time, I was only fifty-four.

6. The sign indicates that it is the entrance to the Ryoanji Rock Garden.

7. Lotus leaves and white clouds float together on the surface of the pond within Ryoanji.

8. The rock garden seen from a wooden floor of Ryoanji, where visitors sit (1)

9. The rock garden seen from a wooden floor of Ryoanji, where visitors sit (2)

10. The rock garden seen from a wooden floor of Ryoanji, where visitors sit (3)

11. A panoramic view of Ryoanji. The tourist information guide reads in part, "The rock garden consists simply of 15 rocks expertly laid out into a bed of white gravel. They express spiritual enlightenment of Zen satori and tell us infinite teachings."

12. The buildings of Doshisha University seen from the outside.

13. A Western-style building on the campus of Doshisha University.

14. A monument in memory of the Korean poet Yun Dong-ju at Doshisha University.

15. The stone inscription provides a brief biography of Yung Dong-ju in Japanese and Korean.

16. A monument in memory of the Korean poet Jeong Ji-yong at Doshisha University.

17. The stone inscription provides a brief biography of Jeong Ji-yong in Japanese and Korean.

18. In the small pond next to the monuments to Yun and Jeong, goldfish swim peacefully as if to express Doshisha University's goodwill toward two of its alumni from Korea.

19. A large Buddhist temple in Kyoto. The sign board reads,

Kosho-ji Temple of the Shinshu Kosho Sect

Kosho-ji Temple was founded by the famous Buddhist monk Shinran. It is the head temple of the Kosho Sect of Jodo Shin Buddhism that enshrines Amida Nyorai (Amitabha Tathagata) as its focal image.

The name Kosho is derived from a phrase expressing the achievements of the legendary Prince Shotoku who spread Buddhism throughout Japan. It sums up the ideal of establishing correct teachings and propagating them.

Kosho-ji became the head temple of the Kosho Sect in 1876 and maintains its role of "correct teacher" and "propagator" to this day.

Kyoto City Office

As the two most important religions of Japan, Buddhism and Shino are crucial to understanding Japanese literary texts, especially those from premodern Japan.

20. A gate of the ancient imperial palace in the middle of Kyoto. In her memoir, *The Pillow Book* (枕草子, *Makura no Soshi*; completed in 1002), Sei Shonagon records some of the events at the royal court as well as her musings on court life. Below is an excerpt from the book:

I cannot bear men who believe that women serving in the Palace are bound to be frivolous and wicked. Yet I suppose their prejudice is understandable. After all, women at Court do not spend their time hiding modestly behind fans and screens, but walk about, looking openly at people they chance to meet. Yes, they see everyone face to face, not only ladies-in-waiting like themselves, but even Their Imperial Majesties (whose august names I hardly dare mention), High Court Nobles, senior courtiers, and other gentlemen of high rank. In the presence of such exalted personages, the women in the Palace are all equally brazen, whether they be the maids of ladies-in-waiting, or the relations of Court ladies who have come to visit them, or housekeepers, or latrine-cleaners, or women who are of no more value than a roof-tile or a pebble. Small wonder that the young men regard them as immodest! Yet are the gentlemen themselves any less so? They are not exactly bashful when it comes to looking at the great people in the Palace. No, everyone at Court is much the same in this respect. (*The Pillow-Book of Sei Shonagon*. Translated by Ivan Morris.)

21. English translations of three books from the Heian period (794-1185):

- Porter, William N., trans. *A Hundred Verses from Old Japan: Being a Translation of the Hyaku-nin-isshiu.* 1909. Tokyo and Rutland, VT: Tuttle, 1979. The poet Sadaiye Fujiwara compiled this well-known anthology in A.D. 1235. The first several poems predate the Heian period.

- Shōnagon, Sei. *The Pillow Book.* Trans. Arthur Waley. 1928. Mineola, N.Y.: Dover Publications, 2019. A contemporary of Murasaki Shikibu, who wrote *The Tale of Genji* (published before 1021), Sei Shōnagon records some of the episodes of—and her reflections on—courtly life in this fascinating memoir.

- Lady Murasaki Shikibu and Others. *Diaries of Court Ladies of Old Japan.* Trans. Annie Shepley Omori and Kochi Doi. 1920. Mineola, N.Y.: Dover Publications, 2003. The anthology includes the *Sarashina Diary* (A.D. 1009-1059), the *Diary of Murasaki Shikibu* (A.D. 1007-1010), and the *Diary of Izumi Shikibu* (A.D. 1002-1003). The imagist poet Amy Lowell (1874-1925) contributed an introduction to the volume (pp. ix-xxxi).

These three books are in my personal library.

22. A view of Kyoto from an observation tower near Kyoto Station in the southern part of the city. The north-south road in the photo is Karasuma Street. Compared with Tokyo, Kyoto has much less traffic and fewer tall buildings.

23. A historical marker at an intersection near the ancient imperial palace.

24. A close-up of the historical marker. It is in Japanese and English. The English version reads,

The area around this intersection is an archeological site named Karasuma Oike Iseki. [Much earthenware] dating from [the] final phase of [the] Jomon period to [the] Kofu period (B.C. 1000-A.D. 600) [is] found here. In [the] Heian period (A.D. 794-1185) this area was a residential area for the aristocrat[s]. Retired Emperor Gotoba had a mansion called "Oshikoji-dono" with a famous garden and a pond. This area continued to be [a] prestigious residential area during the following eras, and became a center of financial business in [the] Edo period (A.D. 1600-1868). The prosperity and bustle of the area is seen along the Sanjo and Karasuma streets where modern architecture of [the] Meijo period (A.D. 1868-1912) still remain[s].

25. Another historical marker nearby. It is in Japanese, English, Chinese, and Korean. The English version reads,

Karasuma dori [Karasuma Street]

This street was known as Karasumaru-koji during the Heian period. Owing to the wars of Onin and Bunmei, it was devastated. [However, it] was reconstructed by Hideyoshi Toyotomi from about 1590. Many mansions of nobles and the houses of commoners were located along this street. Since the Meiji period, it has become a main street of Kyoto with the construction of Kyoto station and the opening of the streetcar line.

1

2

3

4

5

6

7

8

9

10

11

12

13

14

15

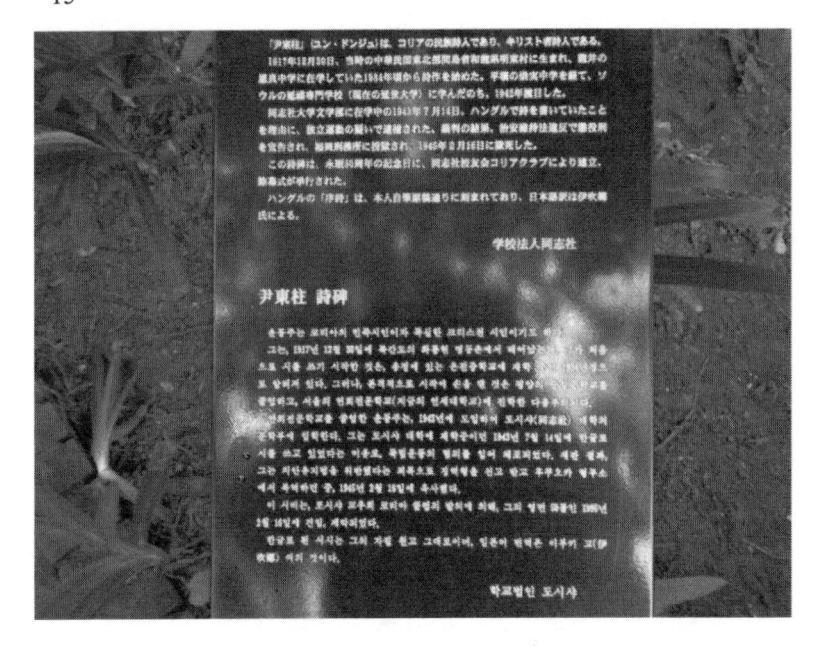

16

17

18

19

20

21

22

23

24

烏丸御池遺跡・平安京跡
Karasuma Oike site / Heiankyo site

この交差点付近は、縄文晩期～古墳時代の土器が多数出土することから、有史以前より生活が営まれていたことが推定され、地名をとって烏丸御池遺跡とよんでいる。

この碑が建つ地点は、平安京では左京三条三坊十四町と十五町の間の三条坊門小路にあたり、付近は当時の一等地であった。中でも交差点北西角の地には、後鳥羽上皇の押小路殿に始まる著名な園池があり、そのために三条坊門御殿などの別名で呼ばれていた。今、ここを東西に走る御池通は、押小路殿の前を通ることに因むというのが通説だが、『拾遺都名所図会』ではこの界隈の園地に由来するという説が挙げられている。

その後も付近は高級住宅地として、足利一門の邸宅が存在したが、戦国時代には、この通りにも堀や城が幾つも築かれ、豊臣の頃には御所周辺を取り囲む御土居が築かれた。それらは本能寺の変にもその舞台の一つとなったと伝わる。

江戸時代になると、金座・幹座などが集中して金融街へと変貌し、その賑わいは、現在でも近代建築の多く残る三条通や烏丸通のオフィスビル街に見ることができる。

The area around this intersection is an archaeological site named Karasuma Oike Iseki. Many earthenwares dating from final phase of Jomon period to Kofun period (g. c. 1000 – c. a.b. 600) are found here. In Heian period (a.d. 794–1185), this area was a residential area for the aristocrat. Retired Emperor Gotoba had a mansion called 'Oshikoji-dono' with a famous garden and a pond. This area continued to be prestigious residential area during the following eras, and became a center of financial business in Edo period (a.d. 1603–1868). The prosperity and bustle of the insurance along the Sanjo and Karasuma streets where modern architecture of Meiji period (a.d. 1868–1912) still remain.

25

Kamakura Museum of Literature

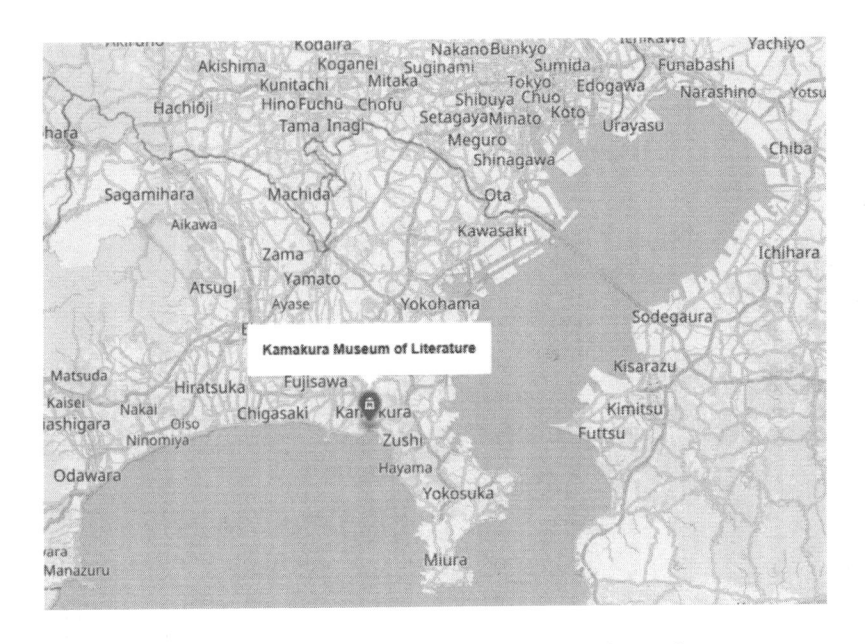

The Kamakura Museum of Literature is located in the coastal city of Kamakura, Kanagawa Prefecture.
Map source: "© OpenStreetMap contributors"

Kamakura (鎌倉市) is a historic city in eastern Japan located thirty-one miles south of Tokyo. In 1185-1333, it served as the de facto capital of Japan (the nominal capital was Kyoto) under the rule of the Kamakura shogunate. During the Kamakura days, the Emperor became a figure head, Buddhism flourished, and the two-time Mongol invasions of Japan failed. Unsurprisingly, there are many historic sites all over Kamakura. When tourists visit the city, they can feel the pervasive presence of medieval Japanese culture. Unlike Tokyo, a crowded megacity in which historic sites are sometimes unnoticeable to the casual eyes, Kamakura is a quiet place where one can see the heritage of medieval Japan everywhere. A number of Buddhist temples, Shinto shrines, and historic locations give delight to those who are interested in Japanese culture and history.

The Kamakura Museum of Literature commemorates a group of well-known authors related to the city of Kamakura, including Natsume Soseki, Yasunari Kawabata (1899-1972), and Yukio Mishima (1925-70). At the beginning of Soseki's novel *Kokoro* (1914), the narrator recalls encountering Sensei ("master") in Kamakura for the first time:

> It was at Kamakura, during the summer holidays, that I first met Sensei. I was then a very young student. I went there at the insistence of a friend of mine, who had gone to Kamakura to swim. [...]
>
> There were many days left before the beginning of term, and I was free either to stay in Kamakura or to go home. I decided to stay. [...]
>
> My inn was in a rather out-of-the-way district of Kamakura, and if one wished to indulge in such fashionable pastimes as playing billiards and eating ice cream, one had to walk a long way across rice fields. If one went by rickshaw, it cost twenty sen. Remote as the district was, however, many rich

families had built their villas there. It was quiet neat the sea also, which was convenient for swimmers such as myself.[1]

The fact that people played billiards and ate ice cream in Kamakura implies Japanese people eagerly embraced Western culture more than a century ago.[2]

Meanwhile, Kamakura once served as Kawabata's home.[3] Born in Osaka in 1899, he began to live in Kamakura at the age of thirty-six. Currently one of Kawabata's relatives owns the house, so it is usually not open to the public. As the vice president of the Kamakura Library, a small company, Kawabata was instrumental in helping Mishima make his debut and gain popularity as a novelist. In *Silence and Beauty: Hidden Faith Born of Suffering* (2017), Makoto Fujimura writes, "[…] Kawabata lived two doors down from one of my childhood homes in Kamakura when I was in first grade. Kamakura became Kawabata's favorite stage as a stage of his lyrical novels."[4] Kamakura serves as the setting for his novel *The Sound of the Mountain*[5]—a story of aging, marital failures, mortality, and the beauty of nature.

Yukio Mishima, a native of Tokyo, met Kawabata in Kamakura in 1946 for the first time, and the two became close friends. During his first visit, Mishima showed Kawabata his manuscripts for *Chusei* ("The Middle Ages") and *Tabako* ("The Cigarette"), seeking his advice. Later that year, *Tabako* was published in *Ningen* ("Humanity") magazine with Kawabata's recommendation.[6] *Tabako* is a story of bullying the author suffered in his schooldays.

Below are the descriptions of the seven Kamakura photos I took in 2007:

1. Kamakura Railroad Station.

2. The entrance to the Kamakura Museum of Literature. Walking on the path toward the museum was a pleasant experience.

3. Another entrance to the museum. The sign on the right side reads "Kamakura Museum of Literature."

4. The plaque reads,

Kamakura Museum of Literature
(A Villa of the Old, Noble Maeda Family)

The house was erected in 1936 by Toshinari Maeda, the sixteenth head of the Maeda family (part of the Kaga clan). It stands halfway up a hill in Kamakura, overlooking Sagami Bay. It represents the villa architecture in Kamakura in those days. Eisaku Sato, a former prime minister and Nobel Peace Prize winner, once made use of it as his villa. It also appeared in a scene from "Spring Snow," a novel by Yukio Mishima, a well-known novelist. The house was donated by the Maeda family to Kamakura City in July 1983. It opened to the public as Kamakura Museum of Literature in November 1985. Main building of Kamakura Museum was registered as National Registered Tangible Cultural Properties in April 2000.

5. The Kamakura Museum of Literature is built in Western style.

6. A rose garden graces the front yard of the museum.

7. As I was leaving the museum, a rickshaw came into view. It made me wonder where it was going and whom it was carrying.

8. The "Great Buddha" statue at Kōtoku-in (高徳院) in Kamakura. Perhaps the most iconic monument in Kamakura, it shows the Buddha in deep meditation on the meaning of life and death. It is thirteen meters tall.

Notes

[1] See Natsume Soseki's *Kokoro* (trans. Edwin McClellan). Washington, D.C.: Regnery Publishing, 1957, pp. 1-2.

[2] In her *Japan Times* article "Ghostly Footprints of the 'Modern Girl' along Kamakura's Coastline" (14 June 2014), Rebecca Milner explains how Kamakura became a popular tourist destination in the Meiji period:

> The origins of this second coming [at the turn of the twentieth century] began in 1868 when the Meiji period rolled around. Kamakura was nothing more than a fishing village, a few days journey on foot from the capital, Edo (now modern-day Tokyo). At this time, Japan had just opened itself up to the West, and along with the influx of Western ideas came one novel idea in particular—the idea that swimming in the sea was good for you. By the time Kamakura Station opened in 1889, things really began to change as the area became much more accessible to Edo residents.
>
> The popularity of the seaside town at this time was partially due to the Meiji Emperor's personal doctor, a German by the name of Erwin Balz, who declared Kamakura to be an excellent site for a health resort.

Several foreign diplomats already had besso (vacation homes) along the Kamakura coastline and as many of the Meiji-era elite followed suit the fashion for kaisuiyoku (sea bathing) was born.

For the entire article, visit www.japantimes.co.jp/life/2014/06/14/travel/ghostly-footprints-modern-girl-along-kamakuras-coastline/#.XfHFJUxFzIU.

[3] Address: 1-12-5, Hase, Kamakura.

[4] For more information, see Makoto Fujimura's *Silence and Beauty: Hidden Faith Born of Suffering* (Foreword by Philip Yancey. Downers Grove, IL: InterVarsity Press, 2016).

[5] Serialized in 1945-54. Edward E. Seidensticker translated it into English (Knopf, 1970).

[6] *Ningen* was a literary magazine published in Kamakura from January 1946 to August 1951. In his book *A Sheep's Song: A Writer's Reminiscences of Japan and the World* (Trans. Chia-ning Chang. University of California Press, 1999), Shūichi Katō recalls,
> At the time when nameless young men like me were publishing coterie magazines and speaking our minds, a number of novelists living in Kamakura pooled their own resources and founded a publishing firm called Kamakura Bunko (Kamakura books). It published a literary magazine called *Ningen* (Humanity). (239)

Katō notes, "Kamakura Bunko began as a lending library and became a publisher after the war. Its founders were Kume Masao, Kawabata Yasunari, and Takami Jun" (239).

1

2

3

4

鎌倉市景観重要建築物第1号　平成2年10月1日指定
鎌倉文学館（旧前田家別邸）
Kamakura Museum of Literature
(a villa of the old, noble Maeda family)

この建物は、昭和11年(1936)旧加賀藩主前田家第16代当主前田利為(としなり)氏が建築したもので、相模湾を見下ろす谷戸の中腹に位置しており、当時の鎌倉の別荘建築を代表する建物の一つです。ノーベル平和賞受賞の佐藤栄作元首相が別荘として利用したほか、作家三島由紀夫の小説「春の雪」の一場面として登場しています。昭和58年(1983)7月、前田家より鎌倉市が譲り受け、昭和60年(1985)11月に鎌倉文学館として公開されました。平成12年(2000)8月、国の登録有形文化財となりました。

The house was erected in 1936 by Toshinari Maeda, the sixteenth head of the Maeda family (part of the Kaga clan). It stands halfway up a hill in Kamakura, overlooking Sagami Bay. The house is typical of the architecture in Kamakura in those days. Eisaku Sato, a former Japanese minister and Nobel Peace Prize winner, once made use of the house as a villa. It also appeared in a scene from "Spring Snow", a novel by Yukio Mishima, a well-known novelist. The house was donated by the Maeda family to Kamakura City in July 1983. It opened to the public as Kamakura Museum of Literature in November 1985. Main building of Kamakura Museum of Literature was registered as National Registered Tangible Cultural Property in August 2000.

設計者　渡辺　栄治
施工者　竹中工務店

鎌倉市

5

6

7

8

Yamanakako Forest Park of Literature

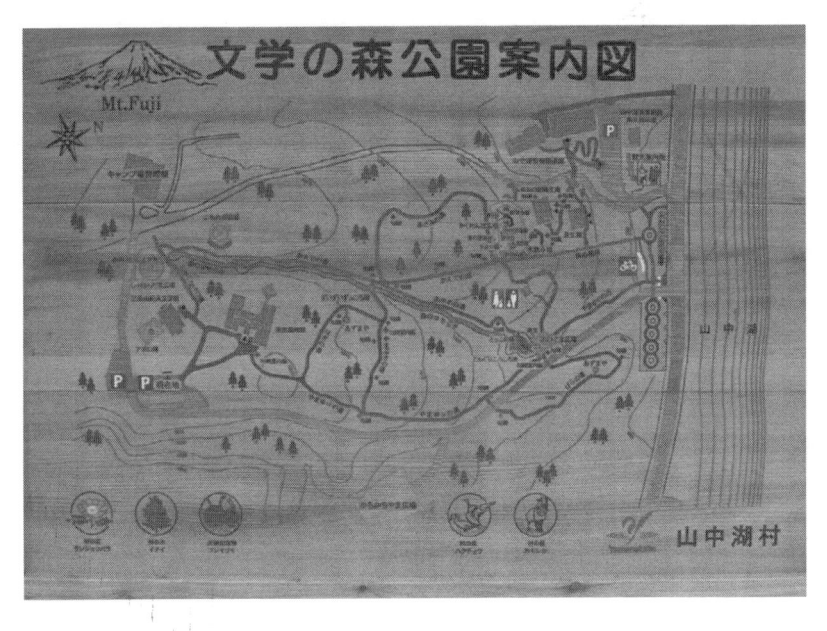

A tourist map on a wooden panel at the entrance of Yamanakako Forest Park of Literature. Photo by John J. Han

After hearing that I wished to visit Mount Fuji, Professor Yuji Kami of Soka University—then a leading Steinbeck scholar in Japan—kindly volunteered to take me there in 2009. We took the westbound train in Tokyo and got off the train at his town. After riding an escalator along the slope of a steep mountain for a few minutes, we reached the plateau, where his neighborhood was. As we entered his house, he introduced me to his wife, who was a quiet woman with a faint smile. After resting for ten minutes, Professor started his car, I sat in the passenger seat, and we departed for Mount Fuji. The peak of the mountain came into and out of our view as the road was winding and hilly. To borrow the title of the country song "Don't This Road Look Rough and Rocky," the way to Mount Fuji was "rough and rocky." The sight of a titillating mountaintop inspired me to write the following haiku:

> way to Mount Fuji
> the foggy mountaintop in and
> out of my view

After driving for half an hour, we stopped for lunch. After eating at a Japanese-style restaurant, we strolled around the area, appreciating the springtime trees, shrubs, and a fishpond. Then, we resumed our journey. Approximately ten minutes later, we reached the base of Mount Fuji.

Our original goal was to visit the mountain, but we soon encountered the sign "Yamanakako Forest Park of Literature." After parking the car, we began to walk on the trail in the park and ended up spending most of our time viewing the literary museums and poetry rocks in the area. In addition to a dozen tanka and haiku rocks along the trail, there were two museums dedicated to the memory of Tokutomi Soho (徳富蘇峰 1863-1957) and Yukio Mishima. A novelist well known to Westerners,

Mishima is also a highly popular writer in Korea. *Confessions of a Mask* (1949), *The Temple of the Golden Pavilion* (1956), *Life for Sale* (1968), and other Mishima novels have been translated into Korean, and the Japanese editions of his novels are on demand in the Korean market as well.

Below are descriptions of the photos from Mount Fuji and the Forest Park:

1. Posing for the self-timer camera with Professor Yuji Kami of Soka University in Tokyo. He kindly took me in his car to his home west of Tokyo, to Mount Fuji, and to Yamanakako Forest Park of Literature in 2009. We had a wonderful day together. Sadly, he passed away in 2016 at the age of sixty-two; I honored his fond memory with a eulogy in Issue 39 (May 2016) of *Steinbeck Studies*. In addition to being an outstanding Steinbeck scholar, he was an excellent photographer. A man with a childlike heart, he had the gift of disarming people with laughter.

2. The sign shows the locations of tanka and haiku rocks along the park trails.

3. A Matsuo Basho haiku rock.

4. A haiku rock.

5. The inscription rock shows a Chinese-language poem.

6. The signpost shows the directions for the Tokutomi Soho Memorial Hall (left) and the Yukio Mishima

Literary Hall (right). Tokutomi Soho was a right-wing intellectual and journalist who supported Japanese imperialism. Mishima was also a right-wing ideologue who dreamed of restoring imperial power; he committed ritual suicide after a failed coup attempt on November 25, 1970.

7. The entrance to the Yukio Mishima Literary Hall.

8. The cover of an English translation of Mishima's *The Temple of the Golden Pavilion*. The copy is from my personal library.

9. The statue in the backyard of the Museum. It looked beautiful, but I thought a statue of a Japanese man—not a Western man—would better fit the purpose of the building.

10. Across from Lake Yamanaka, fog and clouds hide part of Mount Fuji.

11. Professor Kami and I had a picture taken along Laka Yamanaka. Shown in the distance is the foothills of Mount Fuji.

1

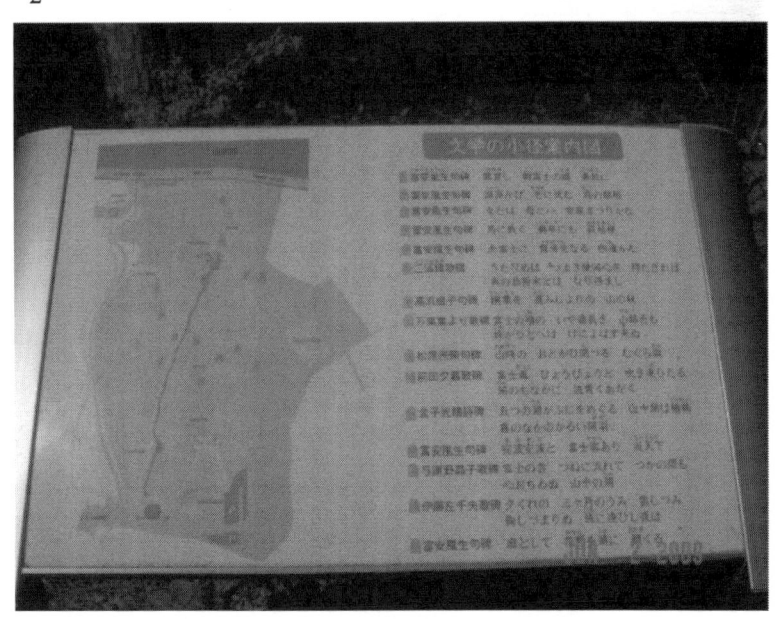

2

3

4

5

6

7

8

9

10

11

Shiki and Soseki Sites in Matsuyama, the "Haiku Capital"

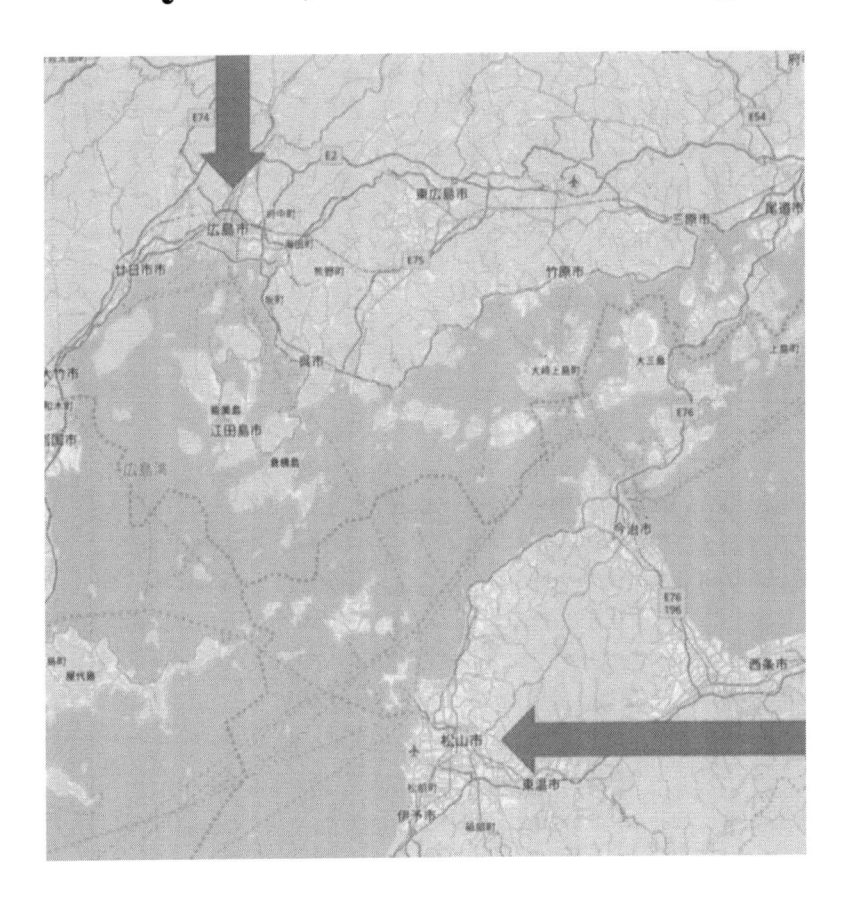

Hiroshima (広島市) and Matsuyama (松山市) are located across the Seto Inland Sea. It takes approximately 70 minutes to reach by high-speed ferry. Matsuyama is on the island of Shikoku.
Map source: "© OpenStreetMap contributors"

It was a long-cherished dream come true to visit Matsuyama (literally "pine mountain"), the capital of Ehime Prefecture, Japan. As a haiku poet and lover of Japanese literature, I had read much about Matsuyama—the home of Masaoka Shiki (1867-1902), one of the four haiku masters in Japan. Matsuyama calls itself the Haiku Capital for good reason. It is the home of many well-known haiku poets, including Shiki and his disciple Kyoshi Takahama (1874-1959), and the city offers many haiku events throughout the year. Fortunately, I took advantage of the annual conference of the John Steinbeck Society of Japan in May 2019, which took place in Hiroshima, to visit Matsuyama. After attending the conference, I took a high-speed ferry that connects Hiroshima and Matsuyama, both of which are port cities in western Japan.

Born to a low-class samurai family, Shiki learned Chinese classics and calligraphy from his maternal grandfather before entering elementary school. After finishing elementary education, he enrolled in Matsuyama Middle School in 1880, but he moved to Tokyo without earning his diploma. In 1884, he entered a prep school for Tokyo Imperial University (present-day University of Tokyo). Six years later, he enrolled in the Department of Philosophy at the university but soon changed his major to literature. After attending the university from 1890-92, he quit school and began to work for a publishing firm while writing and studying haiku.

Although he spent most of his professional life in Tokyo, Matsuyama maintained a strong presence in his psyche. In 1895, for instance, he returned to his hometown to recuperate from tuberculosis for about fifty days; Shiki stayed with Natsume Soseki (1867-1916)—then a teacher at Matsuyama Middle School—and taught haiku to a group of young men. Below are two of Shiki's Matsuyama haiku:

> my Matsuyama—
> the castle tower looks higher
> than the autumn sky

> Matsuyama Castle
> lifted over the mats
> of rice fields

Matsuyama is also famous for sites related to Natsume Soseki. Arguably the most important writer in modern Japanese literature, he was one of Shiki's close friends and learned haiku writing from Shiki. At Tokyo Imperial University, Shiki and Soseki were classmates who had a shared interest in vaudeville theater and admired the literary talent in each other. In addition to writing famous novels (such as Kokoro, Botchan, and I Am a Cat), Soseki penned a number of haiku. One of Soseki's well-known haiku reads,

> Now gathering,
> Now scattering,
> Fireflies over the river.
> (www.poemofquotes.com/famoushaiku/natsume.php)

This poem reflects the poet's keen ability to observe a seemingly ordinary experience and find something profound in it. Gathering and scattering, coming and going, partying and parting—these are part of the human condition as illustrated by fireflies dancing over an ever-flowing river.

The main goal for my daylong trip to Matsuyama was to see some of the representative sites related to Shiki and Soseki: the Shiki Museum, the statue of Shiki in baseball uniform, Botchan Square, Botchan Karakuri Clock, and Dogo Onsen, among others. I managed to see all of them and some more. Most of the sites are on or within walking distance of the square, so it took approximately five hours to visit all of them. The images on the following pages are selections from more than 300 photos I took that day.

    As dusk settled over the square, the crowds began to scatter. They had enjoyed watching the clock move up and down while moving figurines were making delightful gestures. Now it was time to leave for dinner and rest. A rickshaw man who had made some money by giving joy rides looked around and seemed to find no passenger. Standing alone next to his vehicle, he began to sing a slow, high-pitched song. Perhaps he was trying to draw attention from a possible last-minute rider; perhaps he felt bored. Although the song was incomprehensible to me, it clearly had a sad tone; it sounded somewhat akin to "Lover's Farewell"—a high-pitched, mournful song Mother Maybelle Carter masterfully sings (www.youtube.com/watch?v=DYGOdgIR0GI). The man's song inspired me to write the following haiku:

          empty plaza
          the rickshaw man's
          sad song

Soon, it was time for me to take the bus to Matsuyama Tourist Port for the ferry back to Hiroshima. All the way on the darkening sea, the rickshaw man's sad voice rang in my ears. If I had another day to spare, I would have gone back to him to get multiple rickshaw rides so that he could take home some more money.

Photo Captions:

1. A statue of Masaoka Shiki in baseball uniform. As a teenager attending Tokyo Imperial University (present-day University of Tokyo), he played on the school's baseball team. (In 1893, he left the university without earning his degree.) Shiki wrote nine baseball haiku and ten tanka on baseball, all of which are included in *Baseball Haiku: American and Japanese Haiku and Senryu on Baseball* (edited with translations by Cor van den Heuvel and Nanae Tamura. New York: Norton, 2007). Baseball became a school sport in Japan in 1872.

2. The Shiki Museum displays numerous artifacts related to the poet's life, his work, and the early history of Matsuyama. It is a must-visit site for haiku lovers, especially those who cherish Shiki's haiku.

3. On the first floor of the Shiki Museum stand life-size paper cardboard cutouts of Masaoka Shiki (left) and Natsume Soseki (right), who were classmates at Tokyo Imperial University and lifelong friends thereafter.

4. Soseki (left) and Shiki (right) sharing tea and probably discussing poetry. It is one of the items related to the two friends in the Shiki Museum.

5. Shiki died of tuberculosis at the young age of thirty-four. In this scene, displayed in the Shiki Museum, he writes three death poems (jisei) in haiku form on September 18, 1902, one day before his passing. The first haiku is in the middle:

> the sponge gourd is in bloom,
> this *hotoke* [either Buddha or a dead person]
> choked by phlegm

Shiki wrote his second and third haiku on the left and right sides each:

> gallons of phlegm
> too late
> even for water from the gourd plant

> the sponge gourd water
> of two days ago
> wasn't even collected (Trans. in *If Someone Asks…*)

6. Two Shiki books purchased at the gift shop of the Shiki Museum:

   Masaoka Shiki: A Sketch of His Life. Translated and compiled by the Shiki Museum English volunteers. Matsuyama, Japan: The Shiki Museum, 2012.

   If Someone Asks…: Masaoka Shiki's Life and Haiku. Translated by the Shiki Museum English volunteers. Matsuyama, Japan: The Shiki Museum, 2001.

7. Botchan Karakuri Clock on the square. At the top of every hour between 8:00 a.m. and 10:00 p.m., the clock displays characters and scenes from *Botchan* (1906), Natsume Soseki's humorous, satiric novel set in Matsuyama and Dogo Onsen (Dogo Hot Spring).

8. Botchan Train (Botchan Ressha), a restored locomotive that runs between Matsuyama Station and Dogo Onsen Station. The original locomotive ran for sixty-seven years from 1888. In Chapter 2 of Soseki's *Botchan,* the narrator—a new schoolteacher from Tokyo—describes the train as follows:

> I found the train station soon enough and bought myself a ticket. When I got on the train, it looked as dinky as a matchbox. It had hardly started to get rolling when it was already time to get off; the whole ride couldn't have taken more than five minutes. No wonder the ticket was so cheap, I thought—only three sen! (Trans. J. Cohn. Penguin, 2012, p. 16)

9. Famous nationwide, Dogo Onsen attracts high-profile guests, including the imperial family. In the final chapter of Soseki's novel Botchan, a comic scandal breaks near Dogo Onsen.

1

2

3

4

5

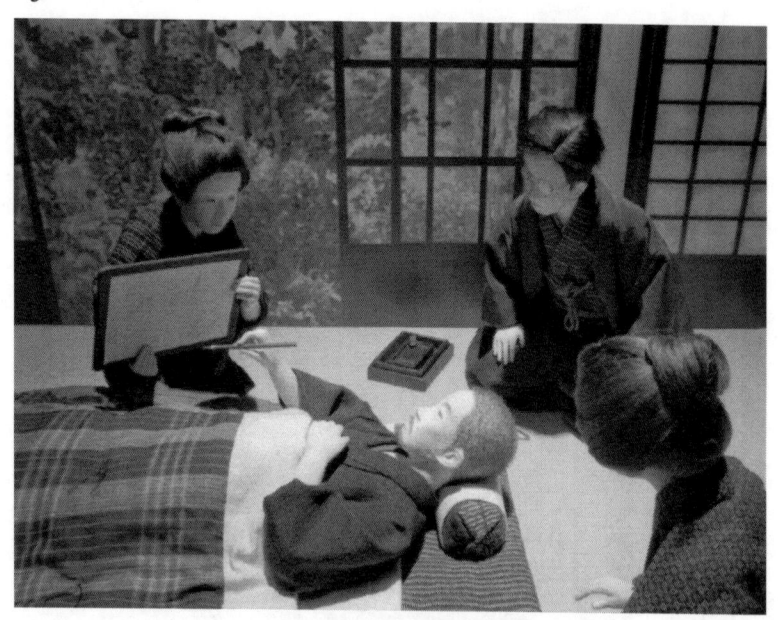

6

7

8

9

Onomichi, Fumiko Hayashi's Home during Her Teenage Years

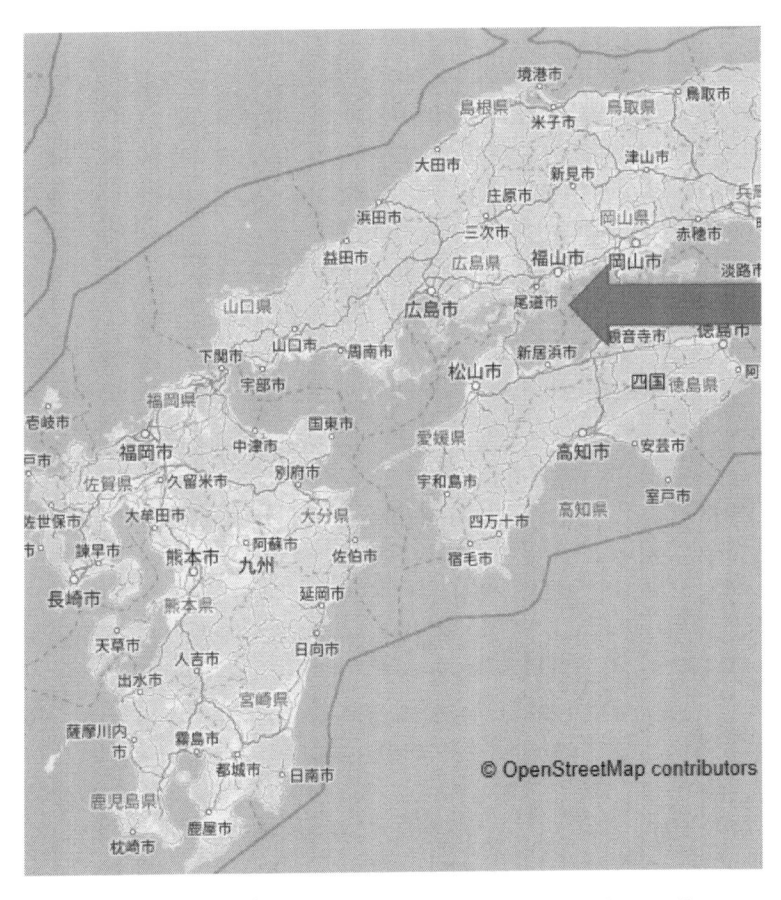

Onomichi (尾道市) is located approximately forty-three miles to the east of the city of Hiroshima (広島市).
Map source: "© OpenStreetMap contributors"

Shinkansen high-speed trains run between Hiroshima and Fukuyama (福山市), where a local train takes passengers to Onomichi. Another option is to take the slow train from Hiroshima and then change trains twice, but it can be confusing for foreign tourists. Train clerks speak English, but it is sometimes hard to find an English-speaking Japanese in the countryside.

*

I first visited the port town of Onomichi, Japan, to see the Path of Literature in 2008 after attending the annual meeting of the John Steinbeck Society of Japan in Hiroshima. At that time, I did not expect to visit Onomichi again. Thankfully, an opportunity presented itself again in May 2019, when the Steinbeck Society met in Hiroshima.

Having visited the atomic bombing sites and monuments in the city of Hiroshima in 2008, I had little desire to revisit those depressing war-related scenes. Accordingly, I took the bullet train east to see Onomichi for the second—and possibly last—time in my life. After getting off the train at Fukuyama Station, I took the slow local train bound for Onomichi. Twenty minutes later, some of the familiar scenes came into view—fishing boats, steep hills that led to the Path of Literature, many temples, and paved roads where traffic was scarce. It was my type of place: far away from the hustle and bustle of the metro, working-class, next to the sea, heartwarming, and nostalgic.

The Path of Literature was my final destination, but I wanted to see first the statue of Fumiko Hayashi (1903-51), a novelist and poet who lived in Onomichi during her teenage years. She was born and raised in Shimonoseki, a city at the western end of Japan's main island. In 1916, when she was thirteen, she and her family moved to Onomichi, where they lived for six years. She enrolled in the fifth grade of the Second Municipal Elementary School and eventually graduated from the Onomichi Municipal Girls' High School.

Upon graduating from high school in 1922, she moved to Tokyo, where she barely survived as a public bath attendant, house cleaner, electrical factory worker, and clerk. After struggling financially for several years, she finally launched a distinguished writing career in 1928—a career she probably had not imagined while growing up in a poor, unsettled family. Her first novel, *Diary of a Vagabond* (1930), sold more than 500,000 copies. Other critically acclaimed novels and short stories ensued. At the age of forty-seven, however, she died of a heart attack related to overwork. Although she lived in Onomichi for only six years, she expresses her warm feelings toward the place in her stories and poems.

Photo Captions:

1. The statue of Fumiko Hayashi on the main street of Onomichi. Her best-known novels include *Diary of a Vagabond* (*Horoki*, 1930), *Crybaby* (*Nakimushi Koz*, 1934), *Lightning* (*Inazuma*, 1936), and *Floating Clouds* (*Ukigumo*, 1951). The following books are available in English translation:

    I Saw a Pale Horse and Selected Poems from Diary of a Vagabond (Trans. Janice Brown. Ithaca, NY: Cornell University Press, 1997)

    Floating Clouds (Trans. Lane Dunlop. New York: Columbia University Press, 2006)

2. Fumiko Hayashi Memorial Hall in Onomichi. Besides displaying resources on her life and works, it sells books by and about the author. Outside the hall stands a cardboard cutout of the author; the end of the hallway leads to a small yard and her home.

3. Fumiko Hayashi's old two-story house in Onomichi. The house displays items such as the author's dresses, her writing desk, and photos from her school days in Onomichi.

4. Some of Hayashi's personal belongings are on display in a glass case. They are part of the Hayashi-related items housed in Hayashi Literary Memorial Hall on the slope near the Path of Literature.

5. The Hayashi memorial rock on the Path of Literature. Inscribed is a passage from her novel *Diary of a Vagabond* that portrays the beauty of Onomichi.

6. The books and postcards I purchased at Fumiko Hayashi Memorial Hall. The two Japanese-language books are a collection of her poems (left; Fukuyama-shi, Japan: Eikou Books, 2013) and a study of her years in Onomichi (right; Hiroshima-shi, Japan: Keisuisha, 1995).

7. A view of Onomichi and the Seto Inland Sea from atop the hill. Although the hill is of moderate height, it has a grade of 45%. Climbing up the steep slope can be arduous and requires frequent stops and hydration. On the way back from the top, I took the cable car.

8. The small diner where I ate lunch and dinner was one minute's walk from the Fumiko Hayashi Memorial Hall. The second photo above is that of lunch. Although the restaurant did not serve dinner, the owner kindly prepared for me a simplified meal so that I did not have to return to Hiroshima on an empty stomach.

1

2

3

4

5

6

7

8

Gems of Japanese Literature: The Path of Literature in Onomichi

The sign reads, "The Path of Literature."
It was a delight to see it after traveling more than
7,000 miles from St. Louis, MO. Photo by John J. Han.

The Path of Literature (文学のこみち *Bungaku no komichi*) in Onomichi, Hiroshima Prefecture, is a destination for many lovers of Japanese writing in and outside Japan. I have visited it twice—in 2008 and in 2019—after attending the annual conference of the John Steinbeck Society of Japan in the city of Hiroshima. The Path is a set of twenty-five natural rocks, each of which has a poem or script by a well-known Japanese author. Some of the authors featured on the trail lived in Onomichi; others did not but had some connections with the town. The fact that Onomichi—a remote seaside town—celebrates literature suggests the high regard the townspeople have for fine prose and verse, as well as their pride in the authors linked to their town.

Onomichi serves as a setting for novels by Naoya Shiga (志賀直哉 1883-1971) and Fumiko Hayashi (林芙美子 1903-51), both of whom are featured on the Path. In Part 3 of Shiga's *A Dark Night's Passing* (暗夜行路 *An'ya Kōro*, 1921), the main character moves to Onomichi to concentrate on his fiction writing. Hayashi's *Diary of a Vagabond* (放浪記 *Hōrōki*, 1927) is an autobiographical novel in which the author relives her six-year residency in Onomichi.

Photo Captions:

1. The starting point of the Path shows the twenty-five rocks that visitors will see on the trail. Selected authors include the haiku poets Matsuo Basho (1644-94) and Masaoka Shiki (1867-1902) and the novelists Naoya Shiga (1883-1971) and Fumiko Hayashi (1903-1951).

2. The Matsuo Basho haiku rock. When I first visited the Path in 2008, it took thirty minutes for me to find this stone marker. I had almost given up on my search

before I found it by accident; it stood right next to where I was standing. On my 2019 visit, I knew exactly where it was.

3. The Masaoka Shiki haiku rock. In 1895, the poet served as a war correspondent in China for the popular newspaper *Nippon*. He composed this poem as he was passing through Onomichi. As I was taking this selfie, several middle-aged tourists from Korea were passing by. A woman said to another woman in Korean, "This is a really famous place. Did you know that?" I pretended not to understand Korean although I understood everything they were saying.

4. Inscribed on the standing stone is one of Nakamura Kenkichi's (1889-1934) tanka poems.

5. A Nakamura Kenkichi monument and his old residence in Onomichi. A tanka poet, he was born in the city of Miyoshi, Hiroshima. In December 1933, he moved to Onomichi to recover from tuberculosis but died there the following May.

6. The inscriptions on the Path are in various shapes and designs.

7. Flowers on the trail helped me pause, rest, and appreciate their beauty as I was climbing up and down the steep hills of Onomichi.

8. Although I normally avoid eating ice cream, I had to buy one after touring the Path and the slopes nearby for more than three hours. The sugary food served well as my pick-me-up.

1

2

3

4

5

6

7

8

In Search of Kawabata's Dancer:
The Izu Peninsula

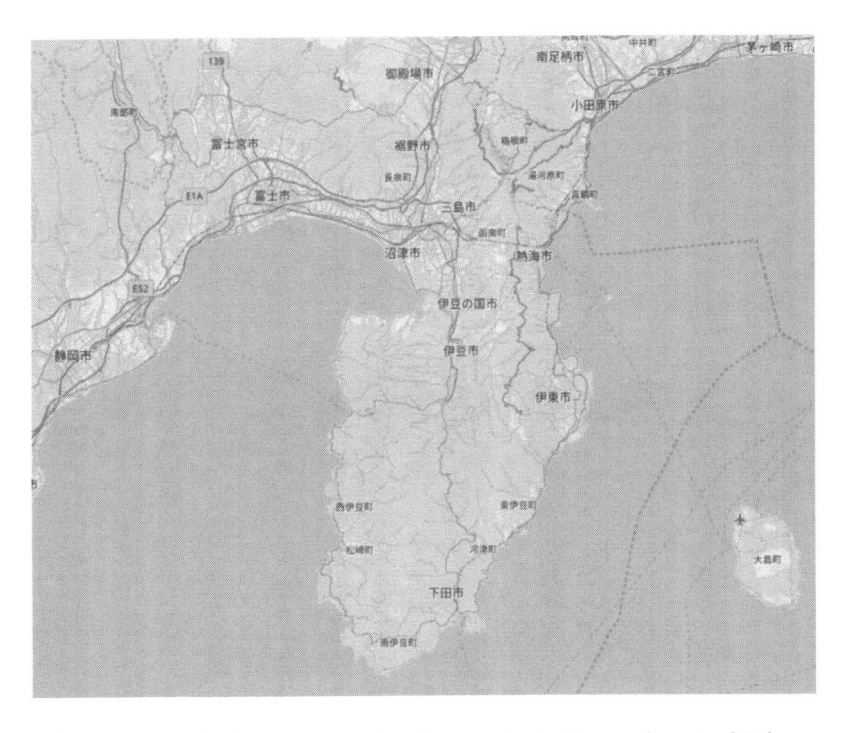

The Izu Peninsula is approximately ninety miles to the southwest of Tokyo. The top of Mount Fuji is visible from some parts of the peninsula. Kawabata's dancing girl and other members of her performing group are from Oshima Island ("Big Island") to the east of the peninsula. Map source: "© OpenStreetMap contributors"

Located 36.5 miles to the southeast of Mount Fuji, Japan, the Izu Peninsula is a mountainous area. Most travelers go there for its hot springs, waterfalls, scenic passes, and charming coastlines. However, I had a more important reason to visit the area in May 2017: It is the setting of Yasunari Kawabata's (1899-1972) short story "The Izu Dancer" (伊豆の踊子 *Izu no odoriko*, 1926).[1] As the 1968 recipient of the Nobel Prize for Literature, Kawabata is widely known for his novel *Snow Country* (雪国 *Yukiguni*, 1948; translated into English in 1956). He is particularly popular among East Asians. For instance, his novels—including *Snow Country*, *The Sound of the Mountain*, *Thousand Cranes*, *The Old Capital*, and *Being a Woman*—are still in print in Korean translation. I remember one of my high school teachers in Korea recommending *Snow Country* as a book worth reading after we entered college. Indeed, Seoul National University recommends *Snow Country* as one of the top 100 books for its students to read.

Yasunari Kawabata (1899-1972)
Image source: Mie Prefectural Art Museum
(www.bunka.pref.mie.lg.jp/art-museum/000219099.htm)

I knew nothing about "The Izu Dancer" until the John Steinbeck Society of Japan announced that the 2017 meeting would take place at Shizuoka University in May. A Google search revealed that the Izu Peninsula is located approximately sixty-two miles east of the city of Shizuoka and that the peninsula appears in Kawabata's story. I immediately read the story and was struck by the melancholy typical of Kawabata's fiction. Finally, after attending the Steinbeck conference, I had an opportunity to see the sites related to the story. The following pages show some of those locations.

"The Izu Dancer" is a short story of unfulfilled love. It focuses on the brief platonic relationship between the narrator—a nineteen-year-old student from Tokyo—and a young girl who belongs to a group of traveling musicians. Initially, the narrator imagines her to be around sixteen but later finds out that she is "a mere child." The girl feels attracted to the narrator, who responds in kind. At the end of the story, however, the narrator decides to return to Tokyo, leaving her distressed yet resigned. As his ship leaves the port, she sits alone on a slope watching him move away from her world:

> [...] The dancer stared fixedly ahead, her lips pressed tight together. As I started up the rope ladder to the ship[,] I looked back. I could see that she wanted to say goodbye, but she only nodded again. [...]
>
> I leaned against the railing and gazed off toward Oshima [Island] until the southern tip of the Izu Peninsula was out of sight. It seemed a long time ago that I had said goodbye to the little dancer. [...] I was no longer conscious of the passage of time. I wept silently, and when my cheek began to feel chilly I turned the sack over. [...] (Trans. Edward Seidensticker, p. 147)

Apparently, the narrator realized that his feelings toward the girl were transient and that he had his whole future ahead in Tokyo; otherwise, he could have promised to come back to her someday. Their relationship was what East Asians would call "unrealizable love" or "unmatchable love." The story recalls the ending of Kawabata's *Snow Country*, in which the male protagonist from Tokyo (Shimamura) has a relationship with a geisha (Komako) in a remote hot spring but decides to return to Tokyo alone.

Although the ending of "The Izu Dancer" will not satisfy all readers, the story expertly portrays the tender feelings of a young girl whose destiny is to travel the countryside as a lowly dancer. It is a story of sadness and sorrow to which readers can easily relate. Although I find the ending of the story somewhat disappointing, it is also a realistic, touching story. There are numerous Asian stories about the romance between two people whose union does not materialize due to their differences in social status. Thankfully, the Izu dancer does not commit suicide as women do in some other stories.

Photo Captions:

1. A view of Mount Fuji on the way to the Izu Peninsula.

2. Typical scenery of the Izu Peninsula. Lush green trees cover high mountains so that travelers can sometimes see only the forests and sky. In the first paragraph of "The Izu Dancer," the narrator states:

   > [...] I had spent three nights at hot springs near the center of the peninsula, and now, my fourth day out of Tokyo, I was climbing toward the Amagi Pass and South Izu. The autumn scenery was pleasant enough, mountains rising one upon another, open forests, deep valleys, but I was excited less by the scenery than by a certain hope. (Trans. Edward Seidensticker, p. 129)

3. A remote Izu teahouse surrounded by bamboo. This kind of establishment may have inspired Kawabata to include the following passage in "The Izu Dancer":

> Large drops of rain began to fall. I ran on up the road, now steep and winding, and at the mouth of the pass I came to a teahouse. I stopped short in the doorway. It was almost too lucky: the dancers were resting inside. (Trans. Edward Seidensticker, p. 129)

4. A statue of the male protagonist and the dancing girl from Kawabata's "The Izu Dancer." It stands in the central Izu Peninsula. In the middle of the story, the girl brings him a bamboo stick as a gift:

> On the far side of the road were bundles of bamboo. Remarking that they would be just right for walking-sticks, Eikichi and I started off ahead. Soon the dancer came running up to us. She had a thick stalk of bamboo that was taller than she was.
>
> "What's that for?" asked Eikichi.
>
> In some confusion, she thrust the bamboo at me.
>
> "For a walking stick. I took the biggest one."
>
> (Trans. Edward Seidensticker, p. 143)

5. The statues of the two main characters in "The Izu Dancer." They stand along a brook and before a waterfall, respectively.

6. The Izu Peninsula is famous for traditional Japanese food—especially soba noodles and wasabi. The best Japanese wasabi grows here.

7. The covers of *The Oxford Book of Japanese Short Stories* (ed. Theodore W. Goossen. Oxford University Press, 1997) and of an English translation of Kawabata's *Snow Country*. The *Oxford Book* includes Edward Seidensticker's English translation of "The Izu Dancer." The copies are from my pesonal library.

Note

[1] Edward Seidensticker's abridged translation of the story appeared in *The Atlantic Monthly* in 1955, and a full version of his translation in *The Oxford Book of Japanese Short Stories* (ed. Theodore W. Goossen. Oxford UP, 1997, pp. 129-148). *The Dancing Girl of Izu and Other Stories* [by Kawabata and translated by Martin Holman] (Counterpoint, 1997) includes the story under a slightly different title.

1

2

3

4

5

6

7

Reader Responses

**Mason Arledge
Clayton Varley
Grace Hahn**

The Threads of Life

Mason Arledge

Saint Augustine once said, "The world is a book, and those who do not travel read only a page." If one cannot make the voyage to traverse the entire landscape of the earth, perhaps the next best thing is to read about such journeys and gaze upon images of the grandeur. By doing so, such individuals can read of Augustine's metaphorical page through a literal one, and Dr. John Han's new book, *On the Road Again: Photo Essays on Famous Literary Sites in Japan,* eloquently opens the door to this type of exploration. In his collection of photo essays, Dr. Han, a notable haiku poet, takes the reader along his travels through the historical literary sites in Japan. While the locations themselves are famous, it is the way Dr. Han masterfully merges different threads and styles through each individual piece that bring his escapades through Japan to life.

Generally speaking, a photo essay seeks to tell a story through images, a travelogue captures personal experiences, and historical writing traces the importance of a person or event. However, Dr. Han expertly weaves together all three throughout his collection of photo essays, complete with precise prose and pictures; he also maintains a strong connection between each individual essay. As exemplified in his book, Dr. Han's travels take him nearer to the lives of Matsuo Basho, Masaoka Shiki, Ichiyo Higuchi, Natsume Soseki, Fumiko Hayashi, Yasunari Kawabata, and other famous Japanese authors. He also ventures to various cities and traces their literary heritage, such as Tokyo, Kamakura, Matsuyama, Onomichi, and the Izu Peninsula. Dr. Han states, "It is my hope that readers will find my travelogues and photos will motivate them to visit Japan and see the sights in person," and he accomplishes this feat by connecting the reader to the sites and works of Japanese writers and pulling him or her alongside his own adventures. Along the way, he effectively combines words—both his and those of renowned Japanese authors—images, and history into a magnificent concoction of life and literary exploration.

    For example, while along the Sumida River in Tokyo, Dr. Han details the inspiration for some of Basho's work and even writes his own haiku in response to the scenery. After snapping a picture of a Basho statue reminiscent of his farewell journey, Han writes,

> facing north…
> Basho leaves behind
> sounds of car horns

Here, he exquisitely ties together the photo of the historical landmark and the life of Basho with his own haiku. In other places, Han employs his poetry to captures the essence of the monument and its history, such as when visiting Masaoka Shiki's resting place:

> Shiki's tomb
> a drizzle moistens his name
> little by little

This instance captures not only the historical importance but also the personal experience of the moment, demonstrating the intertwining of threads that brings the photo essays to life. Thus, throughout his photo essays, Dr. Han employs poems and excerpts of the authors to show the vitality of the places he visits, yet his own haiku also enliven travels for the reader.

    Moreover, several of Dr. Han's photo essays also serve as a brief historical insight into the lives of these renowned Japanese writers and cities. In the essay "A Short Life, a Big Presence: Ichiyo Higuchi Sites in Tokyo," Dr. Han provides a historical account of the life of Ichiyo Higuchi and relates it to the images he captured while on his travels. He creates similar accounts for other authors, but he also details the cities and artifacts and their historical significance, which are emboldened in the pictures. For instance, while sharing of his trip to Matsuyama, Dr. Han knowledgeably recounts the city's relevance to the haiku master Masaoka Shiki. He then includes a photo of a statue of Shiki in a baseball uniform, which serves as evidence for the poet's impact on the location and vice-versa. Similar episodes, coupled with the accurate images, present a historical account of Dr. Han's travels while simultaneously interesting the reader in the historical and literary importance of the statues, hillsides, rustic buildings, and other stops on Dr. Han's literary expedition through Japan.

Lastly, while including tremendous detail on the art and history of his travels, Dr. Han also includes personal narratives from his adventures, which adds the finishing touch to his photo essays. He shares of his own interest and exploration of the famous authors and locations. He also tells of his friendship with the late Professor Yuji Kami of Soka University and of their travels to Mount Fuji; Dr. Han also describes the lonely rickshaw man in Matsuyama. Dr. Han's photos—several of which include him—also add elements of memoir, such as purchasing the ice cream cone after touring the Path of Literature. These snippets of personal experience create a vibrancy in the photo essays and bring the location and authors into modern relevance.

Thus, Dr. Han's photo essays nobly detail his travels, yet they also bring the authors, monuments, cities, and literature to life. His blend of literary recognition and his own poems combined with miniature history lessons and personal narratives create worthwhile tales of endeavors through Japanese literature, which inspired me to write the following haiku:

Dr. Han
travels to Japan
to see literature

Of course, while Dr. Han's writing helps convey his adventures, *On the Road Again* would not be complete without the beautiful and engaging photos he captured along his travels. The broad range of topics included in the images presents a wealth of details and descriptions of the historical literary sites in Japan. When viewing the photographs coupled with the stories behind them, a reader can easily see—through Dr. Han's lens—how the literary prowess of the past can inspire the present.

Mason Arledge is currently a senior at Missouri Baptist University studying English. He resides in St. Louis, Missouri, and has developed a passion for learning in an effort to live an adventure. He is the creator of life2lose.com, a website focusing on personal development, and is working on his first novel. He has published works in both *Fireflies' Light* and *The Right Words*. Mason is also an avid fitness enthusiast with an affinity for sports and the outdoors.

Mason Arledge walking in from the Pacific Ocean while at Coronado, California. Taken May 2019.

Mountains and Fireflies

Clayton Varley

I have never been one for sentimental feelings since the onset of my adult life at 18; in the Marine Corps, I learned that a staple of success in the culture of warriors that I had become a part of was to keep feelings away from my mind. This was evident in the many places that I traveled to while in service. I learned not to become attached, so that when I would inevitably have to leave in a few days, weeks, or months, the sting of distancing myself from something that had grown familiar and sometimes intimate to me would not present itself as sharply. However, in the winter of 2017-2018, I allowed my guard to drop and became attached to something I did not expect to ever feel anything for: Mount Fuji. My unit had been sent to Japan on a Unit Deployment Program where American forces conducted training operations with Japanese contemporary units. These were some of the coldest days of my life. Our unit and our Japanese Defense Force hosts routinely operated in freezing temperatures for days at a time. The one constant that we as warriors experienced was Mount Fuji. Wherever we travelled, the mountain could be seen, and although the peek might sometimes be obscured by towering trees and the grey sky sometimes obscured our line of sight, the mountain was always there. I became attached in knowing that whenever we would begin movement back to our camp where hot showers and warm cots awaited us, the mountain became larger, almost welcoming the frost-bitten warriors returning to its imposing base.

While reading Dr. Han's *On the Road Again*, what struck me personally was his haiku speaking of his journey toward Mount Fuji. I remember gazing up at it from my camp and being awestruck at the grandeur of such a magnificent work of nature.

Though the haiku is brief, the message of anticipation for seeing such a natural wonder sticks with the audience and myself.

> way to Mount Fuji
> the foggy mountaintop in and
> out of my view

Because of Han's ability to effectively convey his message of awe and beauty in such a concise manner, the audience is not left to guess on how experiences made him feel; rather, the haiku serve as a window into a world seldom experienced by Western audiences and provide a "jumping off point" that give readers an opportunity to travel the far reaching wonders of the East. This is no accident. What Han accomplishes with this work is something of noble intentions and worthy of commendation. Most will never get the opportunity to see with their own eyes the magnificence of these experiences as Han has. In recognizing this, and in acknowledgment of an audience that craves the life altering experiences that only travel can present, Han gives his readers a glimpse into a world of beauty. His honorable crusade of giving to his audience what they cannot obtain themselves is worthy of comparison to Natsume Soseki's famous haiku, which Han provides for the audience in his work:

> Now gathering,
> Now scattering,
> Fireflies over the river.

Han is both a gatherer and a scatterer. In this work, he has expertly gathered the experiences of Japan's greatest wonders, given an old Marine a peek at a past life, and effectively scattered these wonders and beauties to the winds to glow in the world as fireflies. Dr. Han's *On The Road Again* inspires awe in—and elicits appreciation from—the audience.

Clayton H. Varley, Jr. is a junior at Missouri Baptist University. He is a native of O'Fallon, Missouri, and grew up in the St. Charles area. He is pursuing a Bachelor of Arts in English and hoping to attend an Ivy League law school with aspirations to become a prosecuting attorney for a major city.   Prior to beginning his higher education, Clayton served in the United States Marine Corps as an infantryman. He was deployed twice and was awarded the Naval Battle Excellence ribbon.

Corporal Clayton H. Varley Jr. (center) posing with two Marines from his squad with Mount Fuji in the background. Taken February 2018.

Keeping Readers Interested

Grace Hahn

Whether fiction or nonfiction, literature can take you to a whole new place in the world. In this case, we are taken across the world through the experience of someone else. This happens multiple times throughout all of the photo essays Dr. Han has created within this collection. In "Gems of Japanese Literature: The Path of Literature in Onomichi," for instance, the Path of Literature is laid before us. Dr. Han takes us through his journey of the Path of Literature and all the small things that he did while he was there. Whenever I am reading a story, or in this instance a photo essay, I can visualize walking through the subject and setting of the writing. Dr. Han displays an excellent depiction of where he was traveling, and it allows you to almost feel like you are there with him.

What is important to me in a nonfiction essay is to have little anecdotes that keep a reader entertained throughout the whole essay. One of my favorite things whenever I read work by Dr. Han is that he never fails to include entertaining bits of information about what his subject of writing is and he helps you get into his mindset. In this case, the bits of information that he includes are about himself and the things he did during his trip. In one instance, he talks about an encounter near a Masaoka Shiki monument:

> As I was taking this selfie, several middle-aged tourists from Korea were passing by. A woman said to another woman in Korean, "This is a really famous place. Did you know that?" I pretended not to understand Korean although I understood everything they were saying.

Including a humorous anecdote like this one makes an informative essay much more entertaining and effective.

In another instance, he talks about buying ice cream after he walked on the Path and the slopes for hours: "Although I normally avoid eating ice cream, I had to buy one after touring the Path and the slopes nearby for more than three hours. The sugary food served well as my pick-me-up." This was another quirky little anecdote that was entertaining to read. After the different explanations and photos of the Path of Literature, we get a fun ending to the essay.

It is fun to almost feel like you are going on the journey with whatever the author has written. To parallel one of my favorite stories, I could compare these depictions to the fairy tale, *Beauty and the Beast*. While I was growing up, that was one of my favorite fairy tales to read. I was brought into a different world when I read that story. It was absolutely magical, and yet it felt real and raw and like I was there living the story. Dr. Han does the same thing in the photo essays that he wrote. Unlike one of my favorite childhood stories, his stories were of real events. However, they were real and raw, making me feel like I was there. Dr. Han's anecdotes and personal references to his experiences were what truly brought me into the story.

Grace Hahn is currently an undergraduate student studying English at Missouri Baptist University. Though she lives in St. Louis for college, her hometown is in Southern Illinois. Her love for fictional writing is what pushed her to become an English major. Grace is also a player on the Missouri Baptist University softball team.

Grace Hahn's high school senior photo taken in her hometown, Lawrenceville, Illinois. Photo date: October 2018.

About the Author

John J. Han (Ph.D., University of Nebraska-Lincoln) is Professor of English and Creative Writing and Chair of the Humanities Division at Missouri Baptist University. A native of South Korea, he came to the United States for graduate studies in 1988 and became a naturalized citizen in 2008. Han is the author, editor, co-editor, or translator of twenty-two books, including *The Final Crossing: Death and Dying in Literature* (2015), *Worlds Gone Awry: Essays on Dystopian Fiction* (2018), and *Autumn Butterfly: Haiku, Senryu, and Other Poems* (2019). He has published numerous poems, as well as hundreds of critical essays and book reviews, worldwide.

Poetry Books Authored by John J. Han

- *Autumn Butterfly: Haiku, Senryu, and Other Poems* (Cyberwit, 2019).
- *More Thunder Thighs: Haiku Musings on the English Language* (Cyberwit, 2018).
- *And Yet, And Yet—: Haiku and Other Poems* (Cyberwit, 2017).
- *Returning Home: Haiku and Other Succinct Poems* (Cyberwit, 2016).
- *Maple-Colored Moon: Seasonal Haiku* (Cyberwit, 2016).
- *2, 4, 6, 8: Poetry and Fiction from the AP Readings* (Salt Mountain Publishing, 2013, 2015).
- *Thunder Thighs: Haiku Musings on the English Language* (Fountain City Publishing, 2010).
- *Chopsticks and Fork: A Senryu Collection* (Fountain City Publishing, 2010).
- *Little Guy Haiku: Life with Bailey, a Maltese* (America Star Books, 2009).

Poetry Books Translated by John J. Han

- *Chuku: Confucian Teachings in Five Characters* (Cyberwit, 2019).
- *My Wife Is Smiling and Other Poems by Oh Se Ju* (Cyberwit, 2018).
- *Four-Character Proverbs: A Primer for Confucian Living in Chinese, Korean, and English* (Cyberwit, 2018).
- *Like Dew on the Grass: Chinese Poems of King Yeonsan* (Cyberwit, 2017).

- *Like the Wind, Like the Water: Korean Sijo* (Cyberwit, 2016).
- *Eating Alone and Other Poems by Song Su-kwon* (Cyberwit, 2015).
- *The Hill of Peace: English-Korean Poems* (Salt Mountain Publishing, 2015).

Academic Books Edited or Co-edited by John J. Han

- (With Clark Triplett and Ashley Anthony) *Worlds Gone Awry: Essays on Dystopian Fiction* (McFarland, 2018).
- (With Clark Triplett) *The Final Crossing: Death and Dying in Literature* (Peter Lang, 2015).
- *Wise Blood: A Re-Consideration* (Rodopi, 2011).

Other Editorships Held by John J. Han

- Editor, *Proceedings of the Annual Midwest Faith & Learning Symposium* (St. Louis, MO: Missouri Baptist University), 2019-present.
- Editorial board member, *Steinbeck Studies*, Fall 2016-present.
- Ad hoc peer reviewer for *Flannery O'Connor Review*, *MELUS: Multi-Ethnic Literature of the United States*, and *International Letters of Social and Humanistic Sciences*, Since Fall 2016.
- Founding editor, *Intégrité: A Faith and Learning Journal,* Aug. 2002-present.
- Editor, *Cantos: A Literary and Arts Journal,* 2007-present.
- Founding editor, *Fireflies' Light: A Magazine of Short Poems,* Spring 2012-present.

- Founding editor, *The Right Words: A Magazine of Nonfiction*, Spring 2013-present.
- Editorial board member, *Wilderness*, Spring 2013-present.
- Founding editor, *Flash: A Chapbook of Micro Fiction*, Fall 2012-Fall 2015.
- Editorial board member, *Faith and Scholarship*, Fall 2013-Summer 2015.
- *Faculty Advisor, The Collegian: Missouri Baptist University's Student Newspaper,* Jan. 2001-Aug. 2004.
- *Editor, UNL Writing Lab Chapbook* (Lincoln, NE) 3.1, Fall 1992.
- *Editor-in-Chief, Hanultari* (Lincoln, NE) 2, Fall 1992.
- Senior translator-editor, Book Division, Current English Publishers, Seoul, Korea, 1985-87.
- Assistant/Associate translator-editor, *The Monthly Study of Current English*, Current English Publishers, Seoul, Korea, 1981-85.